INSIGHT POCKET GUIDE

DUBAI

Part of the Langenscheidt Publishing Group

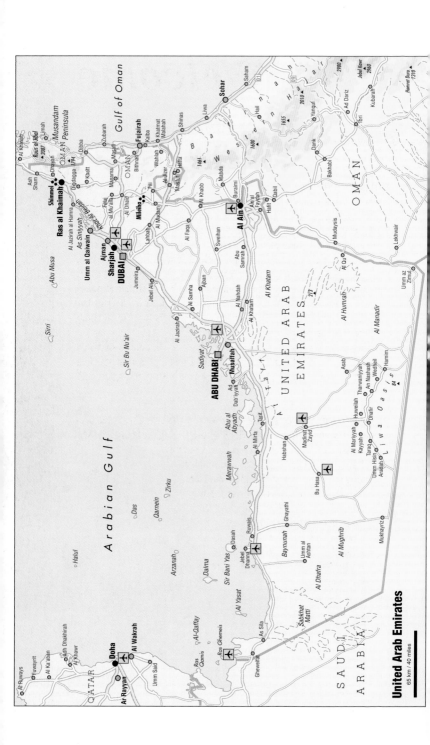

United Arab Emirates

65 km / 40 miles

Welcome

This guidebook combines the interests and enthusiasms of two of the world's best-known information providers: Insight Guides, who have set the standard for visual travel guides since 1970, and Discovery Channel, the world's premier source of non-fiction television programming.

To this end, it brings you the best of the emirate of Dubai in a series of tailor-made itineraries, put together by Insight's expert on the UAE, Matt Jones. It begins with a series of city-based itineraries exploring Dubai's famous Creek, its souks, museums and beaches, and dipping into Dubai's neighbouring emirate Sharjah, now almost a suburb of Dubai. The book then includes a series of excursions to places further afield, including Hatta, with its picturesque fort and hot springs, the wild and isolated beach at Dibba, a 4WD desert adventure and a journey through the northern emirates from Sharjah to Ajman and Umm al Qaiwan, coastal backwaters that still display some of characteristics shared by all the emirates before the oil boom changed them so dramatically.

Supporting the itineraries are sections on history and culture, shopping, eating out, nightlife and a calendar of special events, plus a fact-packed practical information section, with ideas on where to stay, getting around, money matters, etiquette, etc.

Matt Jones, a native of Pembrokeshire, Wales, trained as a journalist with the *South Wales Echo* before joining the Sharjah, UAE-based *Gulf Today* in 1996. A subsequent move into public relations in Dubai saw him handle publicity for several major international companies, but he continued to write in his spare time. He was a member of the team behind *Insight Guide: Oman and the UAE*, and his travel writing has appeared in a range of publications, including the *Daily Telegraph*, the *Sunday Telegraph*, *The South China Morning Post* and the *Japan Times*.

6   **contents**

HISTORY AND CULTURE

An introduction to the region, from the birth of the Babylonians, through the dawn of Islam, to the greed of European colonists and the rise of the Al Maktoum dynasty **11**

CITY ITINERARIES

Eleven tours present Dubai's many faces, with guidelines on local mores, essential sights and renting a car.

EXCURSIONS

Four worthwhile excursions to destinations within easy reach, including into the northern emirates of Sharjah, Ajman and Umm Al Qaiwain.

LEISURE ACTIVITIES

CALENDAR OF EVENTS

PRACTICAL INFORMATION

MAPS

INDEX AND CREDITS

Pages 2/3: reflections of Jumeira
Pages 8/9: night falls over the Creek

History
&Culture

A look at the fascinating, though fragmented, story of Dubai's rise from fishing village to economic powerhouse shows that, for much of the emirate's existence, foreign travellers have regarded it as little more than a stopover on the long journey to somewhere more exciting. To the armies of Alexander the Great, the region linked the battlefields of India with their Mediterranean homes; to the 7th-century Omayyads it straddled a key caravan route; to the 17th-century Portuguese imperialists, and indeed their British successors, it lay conveniently en route to India's riches; to the airline pioneers of the 1930s it was a staging post between London and Australia; to air passengers in recent decades it was merely a duty-free diversion on long, intercontinental flights. In the course of all this history, Dubai seems to have prompted little in the way of admiration. A British naval captain in 1822 described Dubai as 'an assemblage of mud hovels surrounded by a low mud wall'. The eminent explorer Wilfred Thesiger – who found the barren Empty Quarter more appealing – was unable to elaborate much further in *Arabian Sands* more than a century later.

Now, for the first time, Dubai is emerging as a destination in its own right, and is fêted in the glossiest of international travel magazines. The survival and consolidation of the United Arab Emirates (UAE) federation, the enlightened leadership of Dubai's ruling Al Maktoum family, the creation of an impressive, oil-financed infrastructure and the state's encouragement of the private sector, all allied to the traditional strengths of tribal loyalty and religious unity, are creating exactly the sort of holiday destination that Dubai could formerly only serve as a stopover.

Civic Pride

In Dubai, history is not a collection of past events but something that is happening today. Almost two centuries after its mud hovels were summarily described by the officer of the British empire, Dubai is experiencing its own golden age. Dubai is the Tyre of our times, a contemporary Carthage. The sophisticated civilisation that has emerged from a tribal Bedouin heritage is making the desert fertile and building magnificent monuments to itself. Though Dubai's contemporary architectural wonders might not outlast Egypt's stone antiquities, they are built with a similar sense of civic pride and sky-piercing optimism. In contrast with many Middle Eastern cities, the history and culture of

Left: a cargo boat sailing in Dubai waters in 1950
Right: a 13th-century Arab passenger boat

Dubai is not a 'rise and fall' story, but one of rise and rise. A look at Dubai's past prepares the way for a visit to an exciting, dynamic destination.

Evidence of settlements on the Arabian Gulf coast and further inland in the Hajar Mountains dates back to the Stone Age, around 5,000 BC. Among the Neolithic finds uncovered by archaeologists working in the UAE since the 1950s are examples of Ubaid pottery found on the coast – indicating contact between communities there and those in southern Iraq – and arrowheads and hunting tools in the mountains. Historians have concluded that Neolithic agriculture and animal husbandry were well developed in these parts and that people had the time and wealth to acquire personal items. It's also likely that the climate was kinder during this period.

There's further evidence of foreign influences in the Bronze Age, when the region was known as Magan. First mentioned during the reign of Sargon of Akkad (2370–2316 BC), Magan supplied the Sumerians in the Fertile Crescent of the Euphrates and Tigris Valleys to the north with copper. Magan lay on the trade routes between Oman and Yemen to the south and it's possible that some of its inhabitants joined the migration up the east coast of the Arabian peninsula around 3500 BC, when the migrants and Sumerians became Babylonians. Archeological digs at Hili near Al Ain have uncovered evidence suggesting that stable farming communities imported luxury goods, while at Al Qusais in Dubai excavations in the late 1970s unearthed bronze arrowheads, hooks and needles.

Records of Magan dry up in the second millennium BC for reasons that can only be guessed at. Perhaps desertification was to blame, or the decline in Gulf trade following the fall of the Sumerian Larsa dynasty after 1900 BC. It could be that the advent of iron made copper redundant. There are fewer signs of activity in the region during the Iron Age, from 1000 BC to 300 BC, but the relatively small number of archaeological finds from the period suggest that the Bronze Age Hili and Al Qusais sites were reoccupied.

Hellenistic discoveries at Meleiha in the neighbouring emirate of Sharjah, and at Ad Door near Umm Al Qaiwain, reveal the influence of the Greeks in the 4th century BC. It's thought that the rump of Alexander the Great's army passed through the area on its return from campaigns in the Indian subcontinent, apparently scattering pottery as it went.

The Islamic Era

The Battle of Dibba, in around AD 632–635 – little more than a decade after the Prophet Mohammed's *hijra* (flight) from Mecca to Medina – marked the dawn of a new Islamic era. Although tribal wars were to continue for the next 1,300 years, Islam brought the basis of regional unity. Indeed it still dominates the cultural, social, moral, economic, legal and political spheres of life in Dubai. History books do mention various Gulf coastal settlements, but a lot of what we know is the result not only of archeological evidence but of the indigenous population's oral tradition.

Left: Portuguese explorer Vasco da Gama

In the 6th century, Jumeira was a caravan station linking Ctesiphon, in what is today Iraq, with northern Oman. We know that its architecture was initially influenced by the Sassanians (Persians) and, in the 7th century, by the Omayyads. Fast-forward nine centuries to 1580, when the Italian explorer Gasparo Balbi described Dubai, in one of the first specific references to the town, as a prosperous place largely dependent on pearl fishing. It can be assumed that at this time livelihoods depended on conventional fishing and boat building as well as the pearl trade.

For all the prosperity it brought, the pearl trade was responsible for an aspect of Dubai's history that caused much local suffering: it attracted the greed of colonialists. In the 16th century, Portugal conquered the kingdom of Hormuz, which administered the Gulf coast, and occupied Bahrain and Julfar (modern-day Ras Al Khaimah and the supposed birthplace of Vasco da Gama's navigator, Ahmad Bin Majed). The Portuguese dominated the region for a century. By the time they were expelled from Hormuz by Shah Abbas and the British East India Company in 1622, and from Julfar, Sohar and Muscat by the Yaariba dynasty imams of Oman in 1650, they had seized Arab goods, burnt Arab ships and forced Arab societies to leave the coast for the safety of inland oasis settlements. It was not until a political vacuum was created by the collapse of the Yaariba in 1724 that those Arabs who had fled the Portuguese migrated back to the coast from inner Arabia.

The Rise of the Al Maktoums

The dominant tribe at this time was the Bani Yas, from the Liwa and Al Ain oases. Sheikh Shakbut of the Al Bu Falah (or Al Nahyan) branch of the Bani Yas assumed political power in Abu Dhabi in 1793, after which Dubai, with a population of 1,200, became a dependency. In 1833, Maktoum Bin Butti of the Al Bu Falasah branch of the Bani Yas arrived in Bur Dubai with 800 tribesmen and declared the town's independence from Abu Dhabi. The subsequent fighting had an adverse effect on Gulf shipping and, in 1835

Above: a pearling boat heads for Dubai in 1949

Britain, which was less interested in the Gulf's internal affairs than in maritime security, demanded that Abu Dhabi give up the vessels it had captured and pay compensation. With peace imposed, Maktoum Bin Butti consolidated his power in Dubai, extending his influence to Deira, in 1841, and later Shindagha, thereby establishing the dynasty which still rules Dubai.

British Hegemony

While Maktoum Bin Butti was establishing a power base in Dubai, Britain was extending its hegemony over the Gulf in line with its strategy for the defence of India. In what later became the United Arab Emirates, Britain negotiated a series of maritime truces which succeeded in bringing peace to a region previously destabilised by tribal fighting. The truces gave the coastal sheikhs a degree of legitimacy in international relations, and formed the basis for the UAE's formation more than a century later. The treaties also generated a collective name for the independent sheikhdoms – the area became known as the Trucial Coast. The first maritime agreement in 1820 outlawed plunder, piracy and unproclaimed war; the 1853 Perpetual Treaty of Peace stipulated that the sheikhs should not wage war on each other, a suggestion reinforced by a British promise of protection.

In 1892 Britain's desire to assert its domination in the Gulf – variously threatened over the years by the Ottomans, Persians, French and Germans – led to the signing of another agreement with the sheikhs. The Exclusive Agreement prohibited the Trucial rulers from contact with representatives of foreign powers. In return, Britain again pledged to protect the region from external aggression. Backed by the might of imperial Britain, Dubai prospered and modernised. In 1894 Sheikh Maktoum Bin Hasher Al Maktoum encouraged trade through tax exemptions and, by 1903, there were regular British steamship connections from Dubai.

The backbone of the economy was a flourishing pearl industry that, in all probability, originated in the Stone Age. While life was undoubtedly

Above: life on Dubai's creek before the construction of bridges transformed the area

tough for divers, most of whom were slaves, who risked their lives to find the elusive offshore pearls between May to September, pearling brought tangible benefits to society. Beyond the immediate prosperity it engendered, it exposed Arab traders to the modern schools, hospitals and telegraph and post offices of Bombay. Back in Dubai the traders became the modernisers who built schools and fostered intellectual growth. The pearl trade with India also opened the door for Hindu merchants to settle in Dubai.

The Wall Street crash of 1929 and the introduction of the Japanese cultured pearl in the 1930s led to the demise of the pearl industry in the 1940s. For a time it seemed that gold, which had made fortunes for astute Dubai traders in centuries past, would fill the void. Although not mined locally, the absence of customs duties facilitated Dubai's emergence as an important shipment centre supplying India in particular, where the price of gold was fixed at a higher rate than on the free market. But while pearling died and gold soldiered on, the sheikhs were signing agreements that would earn them wealth beyond their wildest dreams.

The Oil Age

The withdrawal from India in 1947 meant that Britain no longer had a strategic rationale for retaining its influence in the Arabian Gulf. But it hung on in the region for another two decades, contributing to its development as never before. Although the security of air routes to Australia was a consideration – Dubai Creek provided a safe haven for British Imperial Airways flying boats from 1937; neighbouring Sharjah opened the UAE's first airport in 1932 – the major factor behind Britain's continued involvement was oil.

Assuming that the oil would soon be found in commercial quantities, the Trucial sheikhs signed concessions with the Iraq Petroleum Company, an international consortium in which Britain had an interest, between 1936 and 1952. In 1951 Britain established the Trucial Oman Scouts to keep regional order – Saudi Arabia had designs on Buraimi – and support oil exploration in the interior. Eight years later, Abu Dhabi won the race to find oil, which it began exporting in 1962.

Dubai's turn came in 1966, when the Fateh field yielded its treasure to Sheikh Rashid Bin Saeed Al Maktoum and a crowd of onlookers. Known as 'the father of modern Dubai', the visionary Sheikh Rashid had already established a framework by which Dubai could capitalise on oil wealth. In 1959 he had completed the dredging of the Creek that had been instigated by his father, Sheikh Saeed, whom he had succeeded in the previous year.

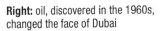
Right: oil, discovered in the 1960s, changed the face of Dubai

Soon after Dubai began exporting oil in 1969, Sheikh Rashid gave his name to the large port being built at the mouth of Dubai Creek. This was followed, in 1979, by the opening of the world's largest artificial harbour at Jebel Ali, which, along with the Great Wall of China, is one of the few man-made structures visible from space. Also completed in 1979 was the ambitious Dubai World Trade Centre project. At 39 storeys, it became the tallest building in the Middle East, and one of the first of many towering monuments that have risen from the desert to demonstrate Dubai's transformation from powerless fishing village to world city.

In 1990, Sheikh Rashid died, and Iraq invaded Kuwait, thereby causing the following year's Gulf War. Far from undermining the progress of the previous decades, the conflict was a catalyst for the further development of Dubai: the city boomed and doubled in size in less than five years. To give but one example of the benefits of modernisation, life expectancy in Dubai has risen from 45 in the 1960s to 72 today.

The Formation of the UAE

Dubai's emergence as one of the great cities of the modern world – fashionable, cosmopolitan and tolerant – has been fostered by the unity of the United Arab Emirates. The only federal state in the Arab world, the UAE was established by Sheikh Zayed bin Sultan Al Nahyan on 2 December 1971 after Britain renounced the maritime agreements of the 19th and early 20th century. Comprising Abu Dhabi (the federal capital), Dubai, Sharjah, Ajman, Umm Al Qaiwain, Ras Al Khaimah and Fujairah, the UAE is headed by a president, who is elected to five-year terms by the supreme council of rulers comprising the ruling sheikhs of each emirate. Until his death at the age of 86 in 2004, the president was Sheikh Zayed, the "Father of the Nation". He personified the UAE's transformation from near starvation to today's centre of astonishing wealth.

Sheikh Rashid was the first vice president and for a time the UAE's prime minister, in which roles he was succeeded by Sheikh Maktoum Bin Rashid

Al Maktoum, the eldest of his four sons. Sheikh Maktoum is also the ruler of Dubai, but it is Sheikh Rashid's third son, Sheikh Mohammed Bin Rashid Al Maktoum, the crown prince, who has inherited his ideals.

In March 2000, he told London's *Sunday Telegraph*: 'I look to the future, 20, 30 years. I learnt that from my father, Sheikh Rashid. He is the true father of modern Dubai. I follow his example.' At the opening of Dubai Internet City later that year he outlined his vision of Dubai as 'the hub for the new economy' based on technology, e-business and freedom of expression. It is with this new focus, away from oil, that he leads Dubai into the 21st century.

Left: Mohammed bin Rashid Al Maktoum

HISTORY HIGHLIGHTS

circa **3000BC** Magan, an area roughly corresponding to today's UAE and northern Oman, supplies the city states of southern Mesopotamia with copper.

1833 Some 800 members of the Bani Yas tribe, including the ruling Al Maktoum family, arrive in Dubai from the desert interior. They set up a principality based on fishing, pearling and trade.

1841 The Bani Yas extends its influence from Bur Dubai to Deira.

1902 Persian merchants move to Dubai to avoid customs duties in Iran.

1903 British/Indian Steam Navigation Company steamships begin calling at Dubai.

1929 The Wall Street crash causes pearl prices to fall. The subsequent introduction of the Japanese cultured pearl sounds the industry's death knell.

1932 The Trucial States becomes a stopover for international airlines with the arrival of British Imperial Airways at Sharjah.

1946 Dubai's first bank opens.

1951 Britain establishes the Trucial Oman Scouts to keep order and support oil exploration in the interior.

1958 Sheikh Rashid Bin Saeed Al Maktoum, 'the father of modern Dubai', becomes ruler of the emirate.

1965 Britain establishes the Trucial States Development Council to contain Arab nationalism and manage development.

1966 Oil is discovered in Dubai. Exports begin within three years.

1968 The first census records a population of 180,000 in the Trucial States.

1971 Establishment of the United Arab Emirates, a federation of seven emirates with Abu Dhabi ruler Sheikh Zayed Bin Sultan Al Nahyan as president and Sheikh Rashid as vice president. Dubai International Airport opens.

1979 Sheikh Rashid becomes UAE prime minister.

1983 Dubai Duty Free is established at Dubai International Airport.

1985 Dubai-based airline Emirates is established.

1988 The Gulf's first championship lawn golf course opens at Emirates Golf Club, Dubai.

1990 Sheikh Rashid dies and is succeeded by his son Sheikh Maktoum Bin Rashid Al Maktoum. Iraq invades Kuwait in August.

1991 The 40-day Gulf war is a catalyst for change in Dubai.

1994 Sheikh Maktoum's brother, Sheikh Mohammed Bin Rashid Al Maktoum, is appointed Crown Prince of Dubai.

1996 The Dubai Strategic Plan indicates that oil will run out by 2010. The Dubai World Cup, the world's richest horse race, takes place at Nad Al Sheba Racecourse. The first Dubai Shopping Festival starts an annual tradition.

1997 The UAE population hits 2.62 million, 70 percent of whom are expats.

1998 The UAE produces 2.3 million barrels a day of crude oil.

1999 Dubai International Airport becomes the sixth-fastest growing airport in the world in terms of traffic.

2000 Dubai Internet City, the world's first free trade zone for e-business, is completed in just 364 days. As a follow up, Dubai Technology, E-Commerce and Media Free Zone Authority launches Dubai Media City.

2001 Following a boom in tourism work begins on Palm Jumeirah, two man-made, palm-shaped islands devoted to hotels and luxury homes. The project is due to complete in 2006.

2002 Leading property developers announce 100 percent freehold ownership for non-nationals, prompting a radical change in property legislation.

2003 UAE population hits 4 million and has the highest growth rate in the Arab world.

2004 The founder and president of the UAE, Sheikh Zayed bin Sultan Al Nahyan, dies at the age of 86.

history/culture

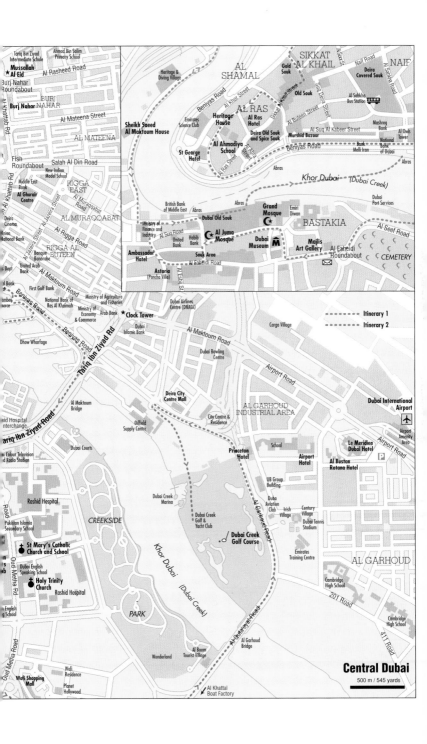

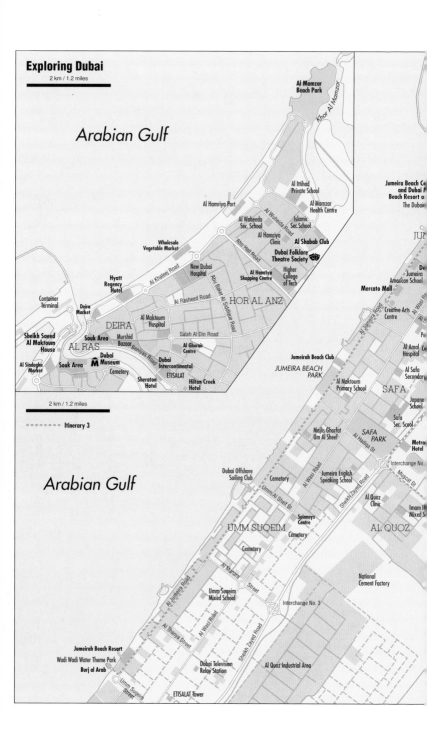

Exploring Dubai

2 km / 1.2 miles

Arabian Gulf

Al Mamzar
Beach Park

Khor Al Mamzar

Al Ittihad
Private School

Al Hamriya Port

Al Waheeda Road

Al Mamzar
Health Centre

Jumeira Beach Ce
and Dubai F
Beach Resort a
The Dubai

Al Waheeda
Sec. School

Islamic
Sec. School

Al Hamriya
Clinic

Wholesale
Vegetable Market

Al Shabab Club

Dubai Folklore
Theatre Society

JU

Abu Hail Road

New Dubai
Hospital

Al Hamriya
Shopping Centre

Higher
College
of Tech

De
Jumeira
American School

Hyatt
Regency
Hotel

Al Khaleej Road

Mercato Mall

Container
Terminal

Deira
Market

Al Rasheed Road

Abu Baker Al Siddique Road

HOR AL ANZ

Creative Arts
Centre

Al Jugeira Road

Pe

DEIRA

Al Maktoum
Hospital

Salah Al Din Road

Al Amal C
Hospital

Sheikh Saeed
Al Maktoum
House

AL RAS

Souk Area

Murshid
Bazaar

Benyas Road

Al Ghurair
Centre

Jumeirah Beach Club

JUMEIRA BEACH
PARK

Al Safa
Secondary

SAFA

Al Sindagha
Market

Souk Area

Dubai
Museum

Cemetery

Dubai
Intercontinental

ETISALAT

Sheraton
Hotel

Hilton Creek
Hotel

Al Maktoum
Primary School

Japane
School

Safa
Sec. Scool

Metra
Hotel

2 km / 1.2 miles

Itinerary 3

Majlis Ghorfat
Um Al Sheef

Al Hadiga St

SAFA
PARK

Interchange No.

Muscat St

Arabian Gulf

Dubai Offshore
Sailing Club

Cemetery

Al Wasi Road

Jumeira English
Speaking School

Sheikh Zayed Road

Al Quoz
Clinic

Umm Al Sheif St

Imam I
Mixed S

Spinneys
Centre

UMM SUQEIM

Cemetery

Cemetery

AL QUOZ

Al Manara

Street

National
Cement Factory

Al Jumeira Road

Umm Suqeim
Mixed School

Interchange No. 3

Al Thanya Street

Al Wasi Road

Sheikh Zayed Road

Jumeirah Beach Resort

Wadi Wadi Water Theme Park

Burj al Arab

Umm Suqeim
Street

Dubai Television
Relay Station

Al Quoz Industrial Area

ETISALAT Tower

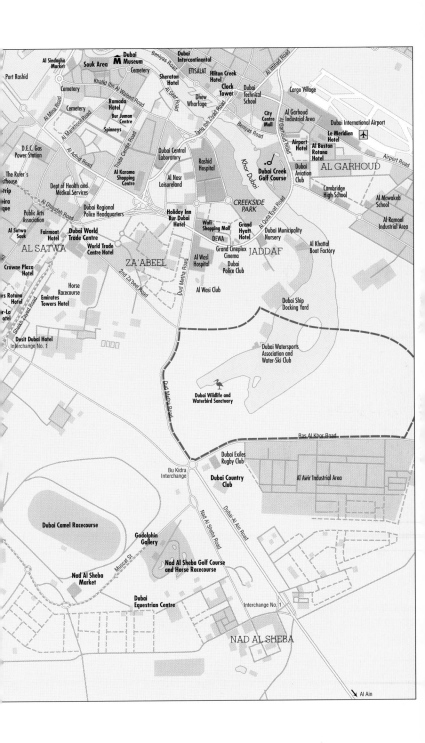

orientation

Orientation

Dubai is contained by the Arabian Gulf to the west and nothing but desert in all other directions. This vast sandy expanse has not limited the city's boundaries – oil wealth, bulldozers and seawater-desalination plants have all played a part in taming the desert. Add land reclamation for The Palm islands project and Dubai sprawls far beyond the confines of its original site.

The sights of both Bur Dubai, the section of the city to the south of Dubai Creek, and Deira, to the north, can be explored on foot when the weather is at its most beautiful (generally between November and April). These walks, with the odd ride in a water taxi or conventional cab, form the basis of itineraries 1 and 2. Don't forget to bring sturdy shoes, sunglasses, sun block and a hat as protection from the elements.

Away from the breezy Creek you won't see very many pedestrians. This is not due to any imposed restrictions on the citizenry – indeed women are making more and more of an impact on life outside the home – but simply because the locals are not much inclined to join the proverbial mad dogs and Englishmen who venture out in the midday sun. Another reason is that, given the relatively low cost of cars and petrol, residents barely need a comprehensive public transport system. Thus for itinerary 3 – and for several of the shorter trips – you will need to hire some wheels.

The first three itineraries link the must-see sights, taking in the Creek, souks and great architecture; the remaining eight explore other interesting aspects of the city, from exploring the best beaches to enjoying a night at the races.

Renting a Car

Renting a car should not present any undue problems. All the big international car-rental agencies have offices in Dubai; there's probably one in your hotel (also see *Practical Information*, page 82, for a list of car hire companies). All you have to do is hand over your passport, your national or international driving licence and two photographs, and the company will organise a temporary Dubai licence for you. You will see some appalling driving in Dubai and so, for an added degree of safety and visibility, it might be a good idea to opt for a four-wheel drive.

The itineraries have been designed to begin at 9am and finish at 5.30–6pm, allowing time for you to freshen up before sampling Dubai's nightlife. It's a good idea to avoid the congestion that prevails during the rush hours. In addition to the morning (7–9am) and evening (5–8pm) congestion, there's a 12.30–2pm weekday rush when public-sector employees head home for a break.

Left: an *abra* captain prepares to cast off
Right: a comfortable skateboard ride at Bur Dubai

1. BUR DUBAI *(see map, p18–19)*

A leisurely, day-long walking tour begins with a look at the striking architecture of Dubai's modern Creekside buildings, followed by visits to the historic wind-tower houses of Bastakia, Al Faheidi Fort, Dubai's old souk and Sheikh Saeed Al Maktoum's House. The tour concludes with a journey in an *abra* (water taxi).

To starting point: Taxi is the only real option. Hail a cab and ask for Dubai Creek at Al Seef Road near the Strand Cinema. If that's not clear to the driver, you might also mention that it's the Creek near the British Embassy or, as it's referred to locally, the 'British Consul' (not to be confused with the British Council, which is elsewhere).

Dubai has undergone drastic cosmetic surgery in the past 50 years. What was once a small, pretty trading village has become a commerce and leisure centre of towering concrete, metal and glass constructions. Much of the new prosperity centres on the wide crescent of **Dubai Creek**. Separating Deira from Bur Dubai, and cutting through the heart of the sprawling metropolis, the Creek remains much as it was in the 1940s when British flying boats touched down here en route to Australia.

It's on the **Bur Dubai** side of the Creek that the two defining aspects of the city are most apparent – the modern, which is kept youthful by enlightened city planners and the avant-garde skills of innovative architects, and the traditional. This tour will demonstrate that, for all the city's fame thanks to its duty-free goods, international sporting events and shopping festival and a fortune gleaned from oil revenues, it still retains many of the characteristics of old, pre-oil Dubai.

The tour begins where **Al Seef Road** nears the Creek before swerving to run parallel to it. On most mornings fishermen – whose numbers represent the many nationalities living in Dubai – gather here and wait for sheirii, safi, neiser, catfish or perhaps even a barracuda to bite. If you stop and chat to a fisherman, he might tell you that few rivers are as abundant as Dubai Creek. Look into the clear water and you can see the shoals pass by.

A Modern Skyline

Look across the Creek and you will see as modern a skyline as you are likely to find on any waterway in the world. If you think that it's impressive during daylight, come back at dusk when the lights are on and the fishermen have been joined by young couples and families. The tall building with the striking convex glass front that reflects the Creek and the passing river traffic is the **National Bank of Dubai**, completed in the late 1990s. Notice how the glass is shaped like a sail – a Dubai motif found on numerous landmark buildings.

Left: paternal care on Al Seef Road

To the left is the **Sheraton Hotel**, with the 'golf ball'-topped **Etisalat Tower**, Dubai's telecommunications company headquarters, behind that. Further left, the second building after the white ARBIFT Tower is **Dubai Municipality**. The **Inter-Continental Hotel & Plaza** stands next to it, while the identical oval towers further down comprise the **Twin Towers** shopping centre and office block.

To the right of the National Bank of Dubai is the blue glass wedge of the **Dubai Chamber of Commerce** building. To your right, the **Al Maktoum Bridge** is one of two bridges that cross the Creek (the other, Al Garhoud, is further on) and, just visible behind that, the distinctive roof of the **Dubai Creek Golf & Yacht Club** suggests a miniature Sydney Opera House. Between the Chamber of Commerce and the Maktoum Bridge are quays around which are clustered dozens of wooden *dhows*, traditional fishing and cargo boats of the type that have sailed to Iran, India and east Africa since the days of Sinbad. The Arabian Gulf is out of sight off to the left, roughly westward.

A Walk Along the Creek

Now that you have got your bearings, it's time to move on. Follow the pavement on your left. You will be heading towards the mouth of the Creek for most of the day. It's about a 4.5-km (2.8-mile) walk and there will be frequent stops for refreshments. Keep your camera to hand as you might well want to capture a visual vignette: a sailor feeding his pet monkey on the stern of a boat, perhaps. You can find shade under attractive Arabian-style canopies. More wooden *dhows* and luxury yachts hug the other side of the Creek. The *Danat Dubai*, a modern sightseeing and dining boat, is anchored at the junction of Al Seef Road and Trade Centre Road (along which you can make out the Bur Juman Centre mall – *see Shopping, page 70*). This is worth remembering if you fancy a 90-minute cruise to, say, the Jumeirah Beach Hotel or Ajman (*see Excursion 2, page 60*).

You soon pass the **British Embassy** compound across the road to the left, whence the sound of birds singing hints at the lush gardens within.

Above: Dubai's creekside skyscrapers as seen from Al Seef Road

(Britain has two embassies in the UAE – the other is in Abu Dhabi, the federal capital.) As you draw level with the Twin Towers, the Creekside path widens into a small park and you can see the tall slender minaret of a mosque ahead. Rising from the Bastakia district of old wind-tower houses, the minaret overlooks the grounds of the **Emiri Diwan**, or Ruler's Court, which serves as Dubai's seat of government.

An Abra Ride

Across the Creek, the Deira skyline is lower now, more densely packed with older bank, office and apartment buildings. **Al Sabkha Abra Station** is in front of the Emirates Bank International. *Abras* are the crowded water taxis you will now see – and hear – in abundance as they put-put up and down this part of the Creek. For a fee of just 50 fils (half a dirham) you can take an *abra* to the Al Sabkha station at sunset. An *abra* ride, in which you find yourself sitting among commuters and shoppers making their way up this timeless water highway, conveys an overwhelming sense of place and gives a good indication of the pace at which people live their lives here.

On this side of the Creek there's been no development immediately beyond Al Seef Road on the left, due to the presence of a large cemetery there. Presumably this graveyard once marked the edge of the old town. As you peel away from the Creek towards the wind-tower houses of **Bastakia**, you enter a district with a rich history. Bastakia dates back to the early 1900s, when fabric and pearl traders from Bastak in southern Iran settled in the area. In building their homes of coral and limestone, they incorporated a feature common in their homeland – the wind towers that have become synonymous with heritage and culture in the UAE. An early form of air-conditioning, these four-sided open towers circulate cool breezes around the interior, while at the same time allowing hot air to rise and escape.

The dense concentration of some 50 wind-tower houses in Bastakia gives a glimpse of what the streets of old Dubai would have looked like in the days before oil. The municipality embarked on a programme to restore these houses in 1996, with the use of traditional materials and techniques. The houses are impressive but anonymous when viewed from the narrow winding lanes that criss-cross the quarter. It's only when you step through the decorative doorways and see the inner courtyards, rooms and balconies that you can appreciate the comfort these wealthy traders created for themselves, in difficult climatic conditions. Especially impressive are the roofs and ceilings, constructed with hardwood from Zanzibar.

Majlis Art Gallery

One of the first Bastakia homes opened to the public was the **Majlis Art Gallery** (Sat–Thurs 9.30am–1.30pm and 4.30–8pm; all day winter; tel: 04 353 6233), on the edge of the quarter on Al Faheidi Road. The Majlis – named after the comfortable, cushioned meeting places under the old homes' wind towers – was established in 1989 and showcases the work of a number of UAE-based artists as well as international artists with UAE ties. It should be about 11.30am when you arrive – a perfect time for a coffee break before you view the oil, watercolour, bronze, glass, ceramic, calligraphic and collage artworks displayed either in the courtyard or in the small rooms around it. The gallery also sells traditional craft items, such as *khanjars* (curved daggers traditionally worn by UAE nationals until the 1970s and still worn by men in neighbouring Oman), goatskin water bags and traditional silver jewellery. Another such house is the nearby Sheikh Mohammed Centre for Cultural Understanding *(see Itineraries, page 52)*.

Step back into Al Faheidi Road, turn right and walk for about 10 minutes to Al Faheidi Square. **Dubai Museum** (8.30am–8.30pm, Fri 2.30–8.30pm; www.dubaitourism.ae) is housed within Al Faheidi Fort, which you can see to your right as you round the corner. The boat in the centre of the square is a pearling *sambuk*, a reminder that Dubai's prosperity has not always relied on oil. Inside the museum, give yourself an hour or so to absorb a history that dates back 4,000 years. The displays explain how life was lived by traders and their families in both towns and desert oases over the centuries.

At around 12.45pm, move forward in time to the streets of modern Dubai. Before lunch, there should be time to wander through Dubai's **old souk** (8am–1pm, Fri 4–9pm). To get there, pass the **Grand Mosque** at the bottom of Al Faheidi Square – one of the oldest in Dubai; you can take a peek inside from the doorway, but unless you're a Muslim don't venture in – and turn right down 54a Sikka. The souk is about 110m (360ft) into this narrow lane. Halfway towards the souk, take a moment to walk a short way up a narrow lane on the right, where a stall selling orange garlands, milk, coconuts and fruit marks the entrance to the **Hindu Shaif Temple**.

Above: a pearling boat at Al Faheidi Square

You might take a few minutes to walk beyond the souk entrance to the Creek: you'll notice how much busier it is here with more river traffic. And there's a fine view across the Creek to Deira's old souk, which features in tomorrow's itinerary. Dubai's old souk largely comprises small textile wholesalers. To the right, about halfway into the souk, you will notice the Dubai Old Souk *abra* station. The station, which links up with Al Sabkha abra station (Bur Dubai *abra* station is for the shorter hop to Deira old souk), is a hive of activity on most days, with any number of the small boats jostling for custom at the steps. Boarding is to the left, alighting to the right.

Electronic Goods

Shortly before the souk divides into two short lanes and comes to an end at 34 Street, keep an eye open for the old **Gray Mackenzie building**, constructed in 1932, to the right. This, the first purpose-built office building in Dubai, was the first base for the city's British agencies and trade missions. Emerging from the souk at 34 Street, take a left turn into an area replete with a vast choice of electronic goods. Now that it's lunch time, head for Pancho Villa's restaurant in the Astoria Hotel. The sign will be visible as you turn right into Al Faheidi Road.

Pancho's, as it's affectionately known among expats, is a legendary watering hole and the Gulf's first Tex Mex restaurant. Primarily an evening venue, it's open for lunch from 1.45–3pm. According to Pancho lore, two American Flying Tiger pilots once phoned from New York to reserve a table. Journalists covering the Iran-Iraq war came here to relax, and in 1987 *Time* magazine quoted a diner as saying that Pancho's had 'The best Mexican food west of San Diego'. Conversely, Bob Hepburn of the *Toronto Star* wrote: 'Pancho Villa's is a symbol of Dubai today: all glitter, all hustle, superficial'. With admirable mastery of the euphemism, this critique was paraphrased in the local press to read: 'The symbol of Dubai's lively, easy going and progressive lifestyle'.

Both versions are displayed on the wall.

After lunch head down Al Nahdha Street towards the HSBC building and the **Shindagha** portion of the Creek beyond it. Much like this morning's starting point, this area has been pedestrianised. The view up-river towards the *abra* stations and the jumble of Creekside buildings is stunning. Once you resume your walk, you will see, off to the left, a smallholding pitched somehat incongruously between the Creek and the busy Al Khaleej Road. Here you'll find a few camels resting before an evening of rides.

Back on the Creek, the dark, multi-storey monolith looming ahead of you is the **Hyatt Regency Hotel**. Its Focaccia is one of the city's best restaurants (*see Eating Out, page 73*). The next stop on the route, **Sheikh Saeed Al Maktoum's House** (8.30am–9pm, Fri

Left: Deira glow. **Above Right:** Sheikh Saaed's house. **Right:** lines and curves on the Creek

3–10pm), is in the foreground. Dating from the late 1800s, this modest home, once that of a former Dubai ruler (from 1912–1958), is now a museum documenting the social, cultural, educational and religious history of the emirate. See the rare photographs that chart the city's expansion from this strategic spot, the wind-towers, narrow staircases and rooms built around a central courtyard.

Further towards the mouth of the Creek is the **Heritage Village and Diving Village** (daily 7.30am–10pm). Featuring re-created dwellings, markets and displays, the villages reinforce the Dubai Museum's historic image of Dubai. The difference here is that you may get to see real people rather than mannequins re-enacting aspects of local life. You'll also have the opportunity to spend your dirhams in the villages' handicraft shops.

Continuing along the Creekside promenade, pass Kanzaman Restaurant, where, in the evening, you can enjoy a Turkish coffee and a fragrant *shisha* pipe, popularly known as a 'hubble bubble'. Kanzaman also serves a mouth-watering array of Lebanese specialities.

If you have the energy to walk for another 15 minutes to the **Customs House** at the mouth of the Creek, assuming it's not hazy, you'll be rewarded with a view north along the coast to the neighbouring city and emirate of Sharjah *(see Excursion 2, page 58)*. Tomorrow's starting point, the fish souk, is across the Creek mouth in front of the new gold souk. Doubling back, head for the *abras*. Ignore the first *abra* station, Bur Dubai; you want Dubai Old Souk *abra* station which connects with Al Sabkha. The 10-minute ride during *abra* rush hour could well be a highlight of your visit. Once at the destination, you will have a panoramic view of the area explored today. Refreshed by a fruit juice from the nearby stall, watch as the sun sinks over the rooftops, silhouetting an Arabian Nights skyline of minarets.

city itineraries

2. DEIRA *(see map, p18–19)*

Traders at Deira's fish souk, gold souk, old souk and spice souk will try to part you from your dirhams during this leisurely day-long walking tour. The *dhow* quays, *dhow* building yard and the greens of Dubai Creek Golf & Yacht Club are among the other highlights in an itinerary that ends with cocktails at the Boardwalk.

To starting point: By taxi. Ask for the Fish Souk in Deira, and to be dropped off in the car park on the Hyatt Regency side of the market building.

While Western consumers are often amazed by Dubai's choice of modern air-conditioned malls *(see Shopping, page 70)*, the city certainly hasn't turned its back on its famous souks. Most of the specialist markets are clustered in an area bordered roughly by the Arabian Gulf, the Creek and Al Sabkha Road in Deira. The souks are vibrant markets where you will see people in traditional dress among those shopping for fish, spices, halal meat and that other Dubai staple, gold.

The day starts at the **fish souk** (7am–11pm) on the Gulf side of Al Khaleej Road. Before venturing inside, wander among the ice lorries parked to the right of the main building. The fish are kept here in iceboxes and either wheeled into the market by barrow-bearing porters or sold to bulk buyers such as restaurateurs. You'll be amazed at the variety of shapes and sizes of fish and, here in the sun, you can appreciate their often stunning colours. Red snappers, belt fish, 1.5-m (5-ft) long kingfish, sardines and baby sharks are among those weighed and tossed into barrows or flat-bed trucks.

Walk parallel to the open-sided main building towards the clusters of people at the far end. Shopping is a social activity –

Above: courtyard of Al Ahmadiya School
Right: merchant and snapper at fish souk

the appeal of this souk, as is the case with most others, lies not only in what is being bought, but in who is doing the buying. Notice the old-timers on the wooden benches, dressed in *dishdasha* and waving walking sticks to emphasise their words; and those who rub their prayer beads before taking the bait and joining the usually good-natured conversations.

In the market proper, walk between the trays of fish towards the sound of chopping at the top left of the hall. Here, buyers can have their purchases de-scaled, filleted and diced by an army of knife-wielding, blue-overalled workers. Next to this section – and definitely not for those of a squeamish disposition – is the smaller **meat souk** (7am–11pm) where skinned goats (the carcasses come complete with tails), lambs (without tails) and cows hang. Somewhat easier on both the nose and the eye is the fruit and vegetable souk (7am–11pm) in the next hall.

All that Glisters is Gold

After leaving the market halls on the Hyatt Regency side, cross the car park and head for the pedestrian footbridge that crosses the busy Al Khaleej Road. Passing now into the Al Ras district of Deira, take a right after the bridge. Ignore the Gold Land building and continue for 450m/yds along Al Khor Street. Turn left on 45 Street and you will see, 90m/yds ahead, a wooden entrance to the covered **gold souk** (9.30am–1pm, Fri 4–10pm). The main part of this famous souk runs along Sikkat Al Khail Street, along which you should

spend the next hour or so trying to resist Dubai's 14-, 18-, 22- and 24-carat sirens. The area's antiques shops are definitely worth exploring, and you can quench your thirst with a fruit juice here, too.

At about 11.15am, turn right out of the Gold Souk onto Old Baladiya Street then first left onto Al Ahmadiya Street: you now have the opportunity to visit two cultural gems – **Al Ahmadiya School** and **Heritage House** (both 8am–7.30pm, Fri 2.30–7.30pm). Like Bastakia and Sheikh Saeed Al Maktoum's House, these two recently restored buildings paint a fascinating portrait of life in old Dubai. Al Ahmadiya School, the first in what is now the UAE, was established by pearl merchant Ahmad bin Dalmouk in 1912. This is where Dubai's future rulers received their education.

Like most of the buildings from that era, the decorative doorway opens into a courtyard, or *al housh*, surrounded by verandas *(liwan)* and various rooms. The courtyard was the place where the children listened to school messages, where they did their exercises, had their breaks, recited poetry and took part in annual events. Moving anticlockwise, you'll see the water-drinking room, the small kitchen, exhibitions on the development of education in the UAE and the school's history, the library, a display of social activities and a traditional classroom. There are more classrooms upstairs.

Above: old-timers relax near the fish souk

Heritage House was the residence of Ahmad bin Dalmouk – after whom a nearby mosque was named – from 1910. The building dates back to 1890 and has changed hands a number of times, undergoing various extensions in the process. It was bought by the municipality in 1993 and has been renovated with the use of traditional materials and methods. The house is now preserved as a lively reminder of the 1940–1960 era which, although relatively recent, belonged to a different world, for oil had not yet been discovered, let alone exploited, in the area.

Returning to the souks, a five-minute walk along Al Ahmadiya Street brings you to Beniyas Road and the Creek, roughly opposite the spot where we were at this time yesterday. The view is superb. Another 10 minutes or so further on is Deira Old Souk *abra* station. Here, cross the road and enter the warren of lanes and alleyways at the bottom of Old Baladiya Street that make up **Deira old souk** (8am–1pm, Fri 4–9pm), an interesting place

to explore for the next hour or so. Notice how shops selling similar items are grouped together: rice and pulses, textiles and clothing, stationery and so forth. The spice souk in the first alley on the left is probably the most interesting section. An amber chunk of sweet-smelling frankincense makes a nice gift.

Life on a *Dhow*

At around 1.30pm cross Beniyas Road and head back to Deira Old Souk *abra* station. From here continue walking along the quayside in the direction of the blue-glass Twin Towers. Now you'll get your first close look at *dhows*, those wooden cargo boats that you have seen plying back and forth on the Creek over the past two days. Their crew members might be busy loading industrial cargo such as vacuum cleaners and used cars, or they might be resting on deck or performing public ablutions in the peculiar boxes strapped to the stern. Don't look too closely.

At **Al Sabkha Abra station**, about halfway to the Twin Towers (where yesterday's itinerary finished), the Creek widens. In the distance, beyond the Al Maktoum Bridge, is today's final destination, the Dubai Creek Golf & Yacht Club. First, though, it's lunchtime. At this part of the Creek the best place to eat is on the balcony of the **Twin Towers'** third-floor food court, where you can look back on the route taken. The cheap and cheerful Apple Café and Restaurant and the Iranian Daniel restaurant, both of which also have balconies, are on the same floor.

At 3pm, continue along the quayside, passing the Inter-Continental Hotel & Plaza on the left and, moored to your right, the hotel's *Al Mansoor Dhow*, which offers a choice of cruises for residents and non-residents alike

Above: Deira's old souk. **Above Right:** a fisherman repairs his net
Right: the *dhow* yard at Al Jaddaf

(see Itinerary 8, page 48). From here, the Creekside car park that has been to your left for several hundred metres gives way to a small but pleasant park. To the left, forming a backdrop to the park's centrepiece statue of a camel, is the Dubai municipality building; ahead, beyond the lawns, you will see a dazzlingly contemporary skyline that features, among its many looming skyscrapers, the Sheraton Hotel, the landmark National Bank of Dubai building and the Etisalat Tower.

For the next 300m/yds or so you will see a variety of sightseeing *dhows* moored to the right. All have sailing times, prices and contact numbers displayed on boards near the gangways.

About 20 minutes after leaving the Twin Towers you'll pass in front of the **National Bank of Dubai** building and the three-sided **Dubai Chamber of Commerce**, which hosts occasional cultural events such as plays staged by foreign theatre companies.

You can see commerce in action at a series of crowded *dhow* quays that point like fingers into the Creek. If you want to see more of the activity associated with these elegant timber vessels, there's enough time to wander out to the tip of quays 2 and 3, where you'll find yet another perspective of Dubai's skyline. Otherwise head straight to the Beniyas Road side of the Chamber of Commerce, where you should be able to hail a cab to take you to your next destination – the *dhow* yard at Al Jaddaf.

At this time of day, the taxi ride shouldn't take more than 10–15 minutes. If the taxi driver knows his way, you should travel over Al Maktoum Bridge, along Umm Hureir Road, skirting the district of Karama (a good place for textile shopping) to your right, and left onto a highway that passes the Wafi Centre shopping mall *(see Shopping, page 70)* and Planet Hollywood

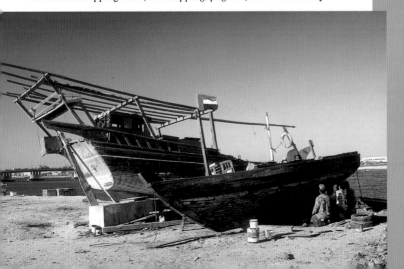

(see Nightlife, page 76). The turn-off for Al Jaddaf is on the right, just before Al Garhoud Bridge. Take the first left – look for the sign to the **Al Khattal Boat Factory** – onto a dirt-track road that leads to the Creek, where you will see a few boats in various stages of construction or repair. Ask the taxi driver to wait; the first 10 minutes are free.

A Marine Playground

Across the Creek you'll see the futuristic Air Traffic Control Tower at Dubai International Airport. To the left of it, above the palm trees, you can just make out the tops of the aircraft-shaped Emirates Training College and the tented Royal Enclosure of Dubai Tennis Stadium, venue for the annual ATP and WTA Dubai Tennis Championships, which regularly attracts many of the world's leading players. The Irish Village, one of the best watering holes in Dubai, is built into the stadium's west stand. Further left is the busy Al Garhoud Bridge and behind that Dubai Creek Golf & Yacht Club. On the Creek you might see jet-skiers or small yachts – for all the industry of the boat yard, here the Creek is a residents' and visitors' playground.

As for the *dhows*, although they look impressive enough in the water, when you look closely at the sturdy ribcage and bones of the largest *al boom dhow* propped up on oil barrels and an antiquated system of wooden supports, you can only marvel that they stay afloat. With the advent of modern materials such as fibreglass, the traditional construction of *dhows* – long planks for the hull, sculpted ribs and beams inside, with oil-soaked cotton to fill the gaps – could have been lost. Such has not been the case. As with

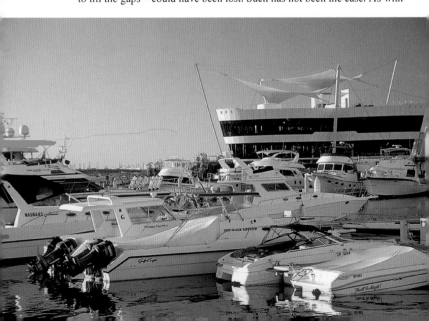

camel racing and other popular local pursuits, the UAE's rulers have stepped in to ensure that their heritage is both protected and promoted. The boats are even encouraged to enter the annual President's Cup Regatta, a race between Dubai and Muscat, alongside modern racing yachts.

The *dhow* builders (*qalaleef*) will happily tolerate your curiosity and may even invite you to take a closer look. These days, most *qalaleef* come from the Indian subcontinent. Their foreignness is somewhat appropriate, given that '*dhow*' is not even an Arabic word – it's believed to have come from the Swahili *dau* – and that the Never-Never Land design of the upturned stern acknowledges the influence of Portuguese traders of old.

Return to your cab and ask the driver to take you to Dubai Creek Golf & Yacht Club. Once again the journey gives you the opportunity to get a feel for the country. Turning back onto the highway towards Al Garhoud Bridge, you will see on the left **Al Boom Tourist Village**, from which *dhows* regularly depart on pleasure cruises (*see Itinerary 8, page 48*). After crossing the bridge you will notice, to the right, the aircraft-shaped Emirates Training College. A right slip road then takes you into an underpass from which you will emerge in front of **City Centre**, one of Dubai's most popular malls (*see Shopping, page 70*). At the traffic lights, take a left, passing the entrance to the Oil Field Supply Centre, from where helicopter sightseeing tours depart (*see Itinerary 5, page 44*), and enter the grounds of Dubai Creek Golf & Yacht Club.

Dubai Creek Golf & Yacht Club
Dubai Creek Golf & Yacht Club is an oasis. One of Dubai's two venues for the PGA Dubai Desert Classic golf tournament, the course was created by

American specialist Karl Litten (who also designed the Emirates Golf Club). The lush lawns and adjoining marina give a real taste of Dubai's wealth. No matter how few travellers' cheques you have stashed away, you'll feel like royalty in this environment. Ask the taxi driver to drop you off at the golf clubhouse. This is the mini Sydney Opera House you've been glimpsing from a distance over the past two days. The club's bar is open to the public and has a terrace that opens onto vast verdant fairways with the Creek off to the right. Walk onto the grass to appreciate fully the clean lines of the building.

You can order tea and watch the shadows lengthen or go back through the clubhouse, cross a lawn that has hosted concerts by the likes of Vanessa Mae and Rod Stewart, and wander around the marina; they say that the old yacht with the funnel belonged to Elizabeth Taylor and Richard Burton. From the marina, head for one of the best spots from which to watch the sunset – the nearby **Boardwalk**. Drink in hand, look west from the balcony to Creek Park and the silhouettes of Emirates Towers and Dubai World Trade Centre, or downriver to neon-lit Deira.

Above Left: Dubai Creek Golf & Yacht Club terrace. **Left:** a crowded marina
Right: sail motif atop the Dubai Creek Golf & Yacht Club clubhouse

3. NAD AL SHEBA TO JUMEIRA *(see map, p20–21)*

Nad Al Sheba Racecourse, the Godolphin Gallery and Dubai's Camel Racetrack form the first part of a day-long driving itinerary that also takes in the Middle East's tallest building, Jumeira Mosque, Dubai Zoo, Sheikh Saeed's summer retreat and the spectacular Burj Al Arab hotel. Remember to pack swimwear because there's a beach stop, too.

To starting point: By rental car. From Jumeira/Deira/Bur Dubai, follow signs to Al Ain then Nad Al Sheba. The racecourse is to the right of the Dubai/Al Ain Road, on the opposite side of Bu Kidra interchange from Dubai

Country Club and Dubai Exiles Rugby Club. A large Dubai World Cup sign rotates above the entrance. Park at the rear of the grandstand.

Begin today's itinerary at 9am at **Nad Al Sheba Racecourse**, some 16km (10 miles) from downtown Bur Dubai. Home to the world's richest horse race, the US$15 million Dubai World Cup, the Nad Al Sheba Club showcases both the city's wealth and its legendary tradition of horse racing. Between 5 and 9.30 every morning from November to April, you can watch Arabian racehorses being put through their paces. Even if you're not a fan of the sport of sheikhs, seeing these magnificent beasts in such a green and pleasant setting is an excellent way to start the day. The chances are you'll be among only a handful of people, to whom the delicious blend of fresh air, birdsong, the whir of water sprinklers and drum of hooves works like caffeine on the soul.

Among the numerous stables and training tracks in the area, those that use the actual racecourse include the Nad Al Sheba, Green, Al Nasser, Moudesh and Maktoum stables. You might strike up a conversation with a trainer from one of them. Aside from the Dubai World Cup, which takes place annually in March, races are held on certain evenings between November and April *(see Itinerary 10, page 51)*. The lounge and terrace of the clubhouse next to the stand are open for breakfast from 6.30am, and its gift shop sells various Dubai World Cup hats, clothes and mementos.

Godolphin Gallery

Behind the clubhouse, to the right of the car park as you approach it from the rear of the grandstand, you will find the **Godolphin Gallery** (Tues–Sat 10am–5pm, 1–8pm on racenights). This small museum commemorates the world-beating exploits of the Dubai-based stables at big races around the world. Godolphin takes its name from one of the three founding stallions

Above: a contestant in the Dubai World Cup is put through its paces
Right: camels prepare for the big race

of the modern thoroughbred. Among those remembered here is the legendary Lammtarra, which in 1995 achieved the historic treble of the Derby at Epsom, the King George VI and Queen Elizabeth Stakes at Ascot, and Paris's Prix de l'Arc de Triomphe, a feat only managed once before, by Mill Reef in 1971. Also on display is the magnificent Dubai World Cup trophy, first won by the American horse Cigar, ridden by jockey Jerry Bailey in 1996.

At around 10.30am jump back into your saddle and drive to the nearby **Camel Racetrack**. Note that, in addition to the road's landmarks, you will be navigating by the kilometres registered on the dashboard odometer, so set it to zero in front of The Godolphin Gallery. Head towards the roundabout with the large Dubai World Cup sign, take the exit to your nine o'clock and you'll see the camel racetrack to your right. Be warned that you might need to stop to allow camel trains across the road. At 2.1km (1.3 miles) turn right towards Nad Al Sheba Market – fodder traders, veterinary clinics and general stores – and park. To get to the racetrack, walk between the shops on the right.

At this time of day you are bound to see several trains of racing camels and their tiny riders making their way back to the stables after training in the desert scrub. They are reminiscent of Bedouin camel trains and opportunities to take photographs abound. The skyscrapers on **Sheikh Zayed Road** present an interesting juxtaposition of the traditional and the ultra-modern. An attractive Arabian tent-like roof covers the grandstand.

Barter for Camel Blankets

Camel races are usually held early on Wednesday, Thursday and Friday mornings and public holidays throughout the winter. If you want to catch one you'll need to be at the track by 7am: the dust is already settling on the event by 8.30am. Before returning to the car, it's worth taking some time to explore the nearby stores. Here you'll be able to barter for exceptionally good-value camel blankets as well as various other items associated with the sport, from whips and muzzles to intricately patterned camel saddles.

Zero the odometer for the next leg at the junction. You're heading for the coast at Jumeira, a 15-km (9-mile) drive away. At this time of day, it should take no longer than 15–20 minutes and there are a few sights to see on the way. Turn right at the junction and you'll see that the road forks almost immediately. Take the left fork (the right leads to the grandstand) and continue on this road until you reach Interchange No 2 on the Dubai-Abu Dhabi Road at 5.4km (3.3 miles). Along the way, you'll see **Godolphin's Al Quoz Stables** to the right at 3.5km (2.2 miles) and, off to the right at 4.4km (2.7 miles), **Dubai Stables**. The speed limit here is 60kph (37mph).

Sheikh Zayed Road

At the interchange, take the right slip road and feed onto the highway heading towards Dubai. The speed limit here is 100kph (62mph). At 8.8km (5.5 miles) you pass under Interchange No 1 and enter that corridor of tall buildings, the Sheikh Zayed Road, that you could see from the racetrack. Ahead and to the right you will notice the twin silver-grey metal-and-glass Emirates Towers, the larger of which is, at 350m (1,148ft), the tallest building in the Middle East and Europe, and the white **Dubai World Trade Centre**, the city's first major building project, which was completed in the 1970s.

You need to follow the signs for Zabeel and Bur Dubai, so keep right. At 11.4km (7 miles) take a right slip road off the highway and at 12.1km (7.5 miles) bear left around the roundabout to the fifth exit, following signs to

Above: skyscrapers on Sheikh Zayed Road
Left: Jumeira Mosque

Jumeira. You're now on Al Dhiyafah Road. Take the middle lane for Jumeira. At Al Satwa Roundabout at 13.7km (8.5 miles), you will see the Rydges Plaza Hotel to your right. The Rydges Plaza's restaurants and bars include the ever-popular Tex-Mex Cactus Cantina *(see Nightlife, page 76)*, which offers a good view over the districts of Satwa and Jumeira.

Go straight across the roundabout, continuing along **Al Dhiyafah Road**. You are now in that rare thing in a city of malls – a pleasant, tree-lined avenue of shops. At 14.2km (8.8 miles), across the lane to your left you'll see the Internet Café (9am–3am, Fri 11am–3am), a superb place to catch up with your e-mail correspondence in the company of a typically cosmopolitan mix of nationals, foreign residents and visitors.

At the traffic lights at 14.3km (8.9 miles), ignore the first sign for Jumeira and Umm Suqeim but follow the second. At the lights at 14.8km (9.2 miles), with the dry docks to your right, turn left into Jumeira Road. Immediately to your right is **The Ruler's Guesthouse**, which hosts foreign dignitaries during official visits, while ahead to the left are the minarets of the fabulous Jumeira Mosque. At 15.8km (9.8 miles), turn right towards Dubai Marine Beach Resort & Spa, and park the car.

Jumeira and the neighbouring district of Umm Suqeim, which tends to be thought of as part of Jumeira, is LA's Venice Beach and Orange County rolled into one. One of the city's wealthiest residential areas, it's home to many of the rich expats who live in Dubai. A sizeable Muslim community lives in Jumeira, hence the various eye-catching mosques. A number of attractions – west-facing beaches (gathering places at sunset), restaurants, cafés, small shopping malls, sailing clubs, a zoo, waterfront park, water theme park and hotels, some of which are truly superlative – draw visitors, from elsewhere in the Emirates and further afield, and create an appealing seaside atmosphere that's far removed from the bustle of the city.

Jumeira Janes and Moscow Beach

The European wives of the Jumeira/Umm Suqeim set are known locally as 'Jumeira Janes', though this disparaging nickname is now almost as politically incorrect as 'Moscow Beach', the name given to one of Dubai's few free public beaches, **Jumeira Beach Corniche**, due to the large number of Russians who used to gather here. The next few hours will be spent in the vicinity of the beach, which is next to **Dubai Marine Beach Resort & Spa**, but there are several options for lunch and activities afterwards.

If you fancy a light lunch, **Japengo Café** in the Palm Strip shopping mall on Jumeira Road offers a fine view towards **Jumeira Mosque**, the most beautiful in Dubai. Or you might prefer to sample the delights of **Gerard**, one of the first European-style coffee shops in Dubai and a perennially popular meeting place for all nationalities, a little way up the road in the Magrudy Shopping Mall. In a converted villa before the mall, the **Lime Tree Café** is an expat favourite.

Right: touting for business

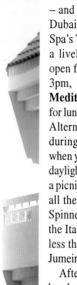

For something more substantial – and expensive – you might try Dubai Marine Beach Resort & Spa's Tex-Mex **Alamo** restaurant, a lively nightspot which is also open for lunch between noon and 3pm, or the resort's **Taverna Mediterranean** restaurant, open for lunch from 12.30pm to 3.30pm. Alternatively, assuming it's not during the 30 days of Ramadan, when you shouldn't eat in public in daylight hours, you may like to take a picnic to the beach. You will find all the ingredients you require at Spinneys supermarket, located at the Italian-inspired Mercato Mall less than 2.5km (1.5 miles) along Jumeira Road.

After lunch, a walk along the breakwater at the end of the beach offers a fine view of the Jumeira skyline, with the ubiquitous commercial towers of Sheikh Zayed Road contrasting with the jolly frivolity of beach life in the foreground. Further up the coast stands today's final destination: the Jumeirah Beach Hotel, voted the world's best by readers of Conde Nast's *Traveller* magazine. Nearby stands Burj Al Arab, one of the world's tallest hotels, built on its own island, and the most impressive landmark in a city of impressive landmarks.

At this point you may like to stay on the beach for another hour or so, visit Dubai Zoo or catch up with the itinerary at Sheikh Saeed's former summer retreat Majlis Ghorfat Um Al Sheef. The following directions apply to all three options. Zero the odometer at the exit to the car park in front of Dubai Marine Beach Resort & Spa and turn right into the flow of traffic. Bear in mind that the speed limit on Jumeira Road is 80kph (49mph). At 1.3km (0.8 miles) the zoo is on your left. To reach it do a U-turn in front of Town Centre Mall at 2.3km (1.4 miles). Just before the car-park entrance at 3.1km (1.9 miles) is a sculpture of stallions that seems to burst through the wall of a villa.

To the Zoo

Despite its small size, **Dubai Zoo** (10am–5pm, closed Tues) is well worth visiting. Originally established as a private collection, it is now owned by the municipality, and its wide variety of animals includes lions, tigers, leopards, pumas, giraffes, crocodiles, bears and monkeys, some of which have been rescued from terrible conditions. Of particular interest are the Arabian species that you're unlikely to see elsewhere, even in the wilderness around Dubai. These include the big-eared Arabian fox, the Arabian wolf – which is extinct in the wild apart from in a few remote areas

Above: a sculpture adorns a house on Jumeira's beach road
Right: Sheikh Saeed's summer retreat, Majlis Ghorfat Um Al Sheef

of Saudi Arabia – and the rare Arabian wildcat, the ancestor of the west's domestic toms and tabbies.

Sheikh Saeed's Summer Resort

At around 4.30pm, leave the zoo, zero the odometer at the exit of the car park area and U-turn almost immediately so that you're heading in the direction of Umm Suqeim. On a sidestreet just after Town Centre Mall you'll see the Creative Art Centre, where Arabic antiques, curios and art can be bought. At 3.6km (2.2 miles) you'll pass the entrance to Jumeirah Beach Park *(see Itinerary 4, page 44)*, which has a very pleasant public beach. The neighbouring Jumeirah Beach Resort is where the England football squad stayed en route to the 2002 World Cup in Japan.

At 5km (3.1 miles), turn left onto 17 Street. **Majlis Ghorfat Um Al Sheef** (Sat–Thur 8.30am–8.30pm, Fri 2.30–8.30pm) also known as Majlis Al Ghoraifa, is a short way along on the left. Originally built in 1955, when the surrounding area was home to little other than date palm groves and fishing shacks, the majlis served as the summer resort of the former ruler Sheikh Saeed.

It's possible that this traditional, two-storey 'meeting place', with its verandas, teak doors and windows and simple comforts was where modern Dubai was conceived, although much credit is due also to Sheikh Saeed's son, Sheikh Rashid, the present ruler's father. The majlis served as a police station in the 1960s but has since been restored to its former glory with the addition of a *falaj* irrigation system in the gardens.

At 5pm, zero the odometer for the last leg of the journey to the Jumeirah Beach Hotel. Turning right from 17 Street into the flow of traffic, do a U-turn at 0.2km and head towards the setting sun. At the Umm Suqeim Centre at 4.1km (2.5 miles) make a brief detour for a superb view of Burj Al Arab: take the right turn into 5a Street and follow the road round to the left to the public beach on 2a Street.

To rejoin Jumeira Road, continue along 2a Street until 4.6km (2.9 miles), when you turn left onto 11a Street. Jumeira Road is at 4.8km (3 miles). At the traffic lights at 6.3km (3.9 miles) take a right on Al Thanya Street for another brief detour to admire Burj Al Arab. Turn left onto the beachfront, but at 7km (4.3 miles) double back until, at 7.4km (4.6 miles), you return to Al Thanya Street and then Jumeira Road. Finally, some 33km (20 miles) after leaving Nad Al Sheba, turn right off Jumeira Road into the entrance for the Jumeira Beach Hotel. Park the car in the shadow of the 25-storey hotel, designed to look like a breaking wave, and head through the lobby for the Dhow & Anchor pub. The day ends with a relaxing drink on the terrace, from which you get a much closer look at the billowing sail-shaped building that is the super-luxurious Burj Al Arab hotel.

Burj Al Arab

Located some 280m/yds offshore and reached via a private causeway, **Burj Al Arab** ('Arabian Tower') is, at 321m (1,053ft), taller than Paris's Eiffel Tower and a mere 60m (200ft) shorter than the Empire State Building in New York.

Opened in 1999 and already an icon, this incredible feat of engineering boasts 28 double-height storeys (all 202 suites are duplexes) behind a sail facade. Constructed with double-Teflon-coated glass fibre, the sail is dazzling white by day; in the evening it becomes, as you'll soon see, an extraordinary canvas for spectacular light displays.

Above: frisbees at sunset
Left: Burj Al Arab, Jumeira

4. BEST BEACHES *(see map, p20–21)*

Take time out to sample some of Dubai's best beaches.

Dubai's Arabian Gulf coastline, with its palm-fringed golden sands and azure waters, is one of the city's major draws. Indeed the beaches' outstanding quality invites comparisons with the shores of some of the world's finest resorts. With the exception of Al Mamzar Beach Park on the northeastern border with Sharjah, Dubai's beaches are located southwest of the Creek, stretching for tens of kilometres between Port Rashid and Jebel Ali, beside the suburbs of Jumeira and Umm Suqeim.

Dubai doesn't have a picturesque, Mediterranean-style coast. Here the Gulf coastline is straight and flat. There are no sweeping bays and the only elevated views are from hotel rooms and restaurants. It's not exactly unspoilt, either. Umm Suqeim in particular is becoming increasingly developed, with new hotels and resorts at various stages of construction. Most of the beaches have been carefully manicured, with trees, lawns or breakwaters added to enhance their appeal. Generally the beaches aren't as wild as those on the UAE's more rugged Arabian Sea coast *(see Excursion 2, page 58)*.

Midnight Dips

Tamed as they are, Dubai's beaches certainly deliver the rest and relaxation promised in tourist brochures, in an environment that meets virtually every holiday maker's requirements: this is the place to bask under a reliable sun with a refreshing drink, and to be pampered in unaccustomed luxury. The beaches are clean, safe and seldom overcrowded. At times they can seem magical: go for a midnight dip for the opportunity to observe the luminescence of microscopic sea creatures that give off a blue-green light when disturbed.

All the hotels on the coast – the Sheraton Jumeirah Beach, the Hilton Dubai Jumeirah, the Oasis Beach, the Ritz-Carlton Dubai, Le Meridien Jumeirah Beach, Le Meridien Mina Seyahi, the Jumeirah Beach Hotel, Sun International's opulent Royal Mirage – have their own beaches.

Even landlocked hotels like the World Trade Centre Hotel have their own coast resorts. (One of the best, the Jumeirah Beach Club on Beach Road, is a favourite weekend retreat for wealthy residents as well as visitors.) Even if you aren't a guest, most of these hotels will allow you to use their beach facilities on a daily basis at reasonable rates. Alternatively, you can visit one of Dubai's public beaches which, with their mix of nationalities and wide range of income groups, are more representative of the city. On weekends and public holidays these places become focal points for popular events such as family barbecues and kite-flying festivals.

Above: the opulent grounds of the Royal Mirage Hotel at dusk

Cultural Considerations

Al Mamzar Beach Park (8am–10.30pm, Thur and Fri 8am–11.30pm; Wed women only) in the city's northern Hamriya district has sheltered, man-made bays, and private chalets for hire on a daily basis. **Jumeira Beach Park** (Sat–Thurs 8am–11.30pm, Fri 8am–11pm; Sat women only), near the Jumeirah Beach Club, is smaller but arguably has the most attractive stretch of palm-fringed sands in Dubai. Both parks charge nominal admission fees. Though restrictions are minimal – beachwear is skimpy, for example – cultural considerations include special days for women and young children and, during Ramadan, changes in opening times and the absence of refreshments.

Jumeira Beach Corniche is the nearest Dubai has to a European-style beach. The promenade at 'Moscow Beach', as it used to be known, stretches for 800m/yds just off Beach Road. Entrance is free and unlimited *(see Itinerary 3, page 39)*. Not a beach as such, **Wild Wadi Water Theme Park** (11am–7pm; www.wild-wadi-water-theme-park.com) is a great, if expensive, place for seaside frolics. Situated in the Jumeira Beach Resort complex, this 4.85-hectare (12-acre) venue is marketed as the world's most advanced water adventure theme park. Themed around the Arabian Nights-style adventures of a shipwrecked seafarer called Juha, 24 inter-connected rides run for 1.7km (1 mile). Highlights include the **Jumeira Sceirah** on which you drop 32m (106ft) and achieve speeds of up to 80kph (49mph).

A final word of warning: Dubai's beaches can have a strong undertow, even in the shallows, and drownings do occur. Unless you are a particularly strong swimmer, save the beach for basking and opt to swim in the beachside pool.

5. A HELICOPTER TOUR *(see map, p18–19)*

The most exciting way to see Dubai in one swoop is by helicopter.

The experience of sitting in a Bell 206 and seeing the city's sights pass by through the perspex under your feet is like taking a ride out of the city centre and along the coast in a great glass elevator. The perfect punctuation mark after the three one-day itineraries, it encompasses virtually every-

thing you will have seen and puts the routes you've covered into perspective.

Aerogulf Services (tel: 04 220 0331, fax: 04 220 0828), a Dubai International Airport-based company that specialises in both oil-industry work and sightseeing trips, offers city tours on Saturdays. At Dhs 975 for the 10-minute trip and Dhs 1,950 for the 20-minute version, they don't come cheap, but with the cost split between a maximum of four passengers they represent excellent value. Tours depart from the quayside of the **Oilfield Supply Centre** on the

Creek between Maktoum Bridge and Dubai Creek Golf & Yacht Club. Bookings must be made three days in advance and all passports faxed ahead. Any time of day is good for such an exhilarating ride, but it's a good idea to take a mid-morning flight so that you have the rest of the day in which to come down from the high and let the experience sink in.

The 10-minute tour heads down the Creek towards the mouth, with Sharjah in the distance and Deira (Dubai Chamber of Commerce, National Bank of Dubai, Deira Old Souk, Al Ahmadiya School) to the right; Bur Dubai (Ruler's Court, Bastakia, Al Faheidi Fortress, Dubai Old Souk, Sheikh Saeed Al Maktoum's House) to the left. Banking to the left at the Creek mouth, you'll have a bird's eye view of Port Rashid, which handles the largest oil tankers, before flying along the Jumeira coastline. Look out for Jumeira Mosque, Jumeira Beach Corniche, Dubai Zoo and Jumeira Park.

The helicopter turns inland at Safa Park (if it's clear you might see the Hajar Mountains in the distance) and, after turning left over the Dubai-Abu Dhabi Highway, flies over Sheikh Zayed Road (notice the many rooftop swimming pools and helipads) before crossing the Creek and landing at the Oilfield Supply Centre.

A Tailor-made Tour

Typically, the 20-minute tour follows the route of the first but continues along the Jumeira coast to the Jumeirah Beach Hotel and Burj Al Arab, the sight of which alone justifies the additional expense. You'll also get to see the camel racetrack before completing the sightseeing circuit by rejoining the Creek above Al Khor and descending past Dubai Creek Golf & Yacht Club and the Boardwalk. Alternatively, it should be possible to arrange a tour tailored to more specific needs. Aerogulf Services helicopters can be booked for flights over the desert to Hatta, for example. If you want a tour on any day other than Saturday, the minimum trip is 30 minutes (Dhs 2,925).

Left: an aerial view, with Bur Dubai on the left, Deira on the right
Above: back on terra firma

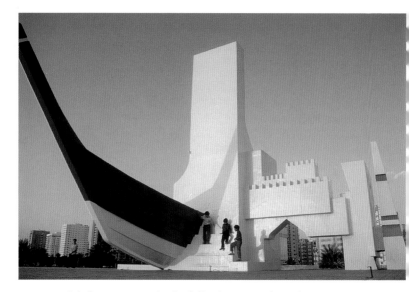

It is important to take the following precautions: don't approach the helicopter until the pilot or a member of the ground staff gives the thumbs up; always approach the helicopter from the front; don't go near the tail boom; secure loose objects and hats and don't try to retrieve any that are swept away. Don't smoke, and don't forget your camera.

6. PARKS *(see map, p20–21)*

Join Dubai's residents at rest and play in the city's beautiful parks.

If you have followed the first three itineraries that linked the essential sights, and visited the souks and shopping malls, but feel cocooned from Dubai life, you might visit one of the parks (small entrance fees). In addition to their sandy shores, Al Mamzar Beach Park and Jumeira Beach Park *(see Itinerary 4, page 44)*, have other attractive features. Spread over 100 ha (244 acres) of a Sharjah-facing promontory, Al Mamzar is the only park in Dubai to have swimming pools. It also has a *barasti* (palm frond) café, picnic and barbecue sites, children's play areas and an open-air amphitheatre that hosts concerts on public holidays and during the Dubai Shopping Festival. Outside these times, the park rarely feels crowded. Jumeira Beach Park is only 12 ha (30 acres), but its compactness makes it seem all the more verdant.

Fairground Attractions

Dubai's oldest park is stituated a little way inland from Jumeira Beach Park, between Al Wasl Road and Sheikh Zayed Road. Established in 1975, the 64-ha (158-acre) **Safa Park** (Sat–Thurs 8am–11pm, Fri 8am–11.30pm) is a particular favourite with joggers and local youngsters drawn by its fairground attractions, which include an electronic-games arcade, bumper-car rides and ferris wheel. It also has some 20 barbecue sites, courts for tennis,

Above: a park sculpture near Khalid Lagoon in neighbouring Sharjah

volleyball and basketball, and a football pitch. Large expanses of grass, small hills and a lake with a waterfall offer greater solitude.

Perhaps the best park within the city limits is **Creekside Park** (daily 8am–10.30pm), an expansive green area boasting more than 280 botanical species that hugs the Creek for the 2.6-km (1.6-mile) stretch between the Al Maktoum and Al Garhoud bridges. Creekside Park offers a pleasant view across the water to Dubai Creek Golf & Yacht Club, its open-air amphitheatre seats 1,000, and it hosts spectacular laser and firework shows during the shopping festival *(see Shopping, page 69)*. In early 2000 it opened the UAE's first cable car system, which rises 30m (98ft) high.

Another fun way to see the park's 90-odd ha (222 acres) is by bicycle-car, which can be rented for a small fee at Gate 2. Like the other parks, Creekside gets busy at weekends and during holidays.

7. FLAMINGO WATCH *(see map, p20–21)*

A morning visit to Dubai Wildlife and Waterbird Sanctuary at Al Khor.

Dubai's flamingo population can be found in the city's sole nature reserve, **Dubai Wildlife and Waterbird Sanctuary**, at the southern end of the Creek. It can be reached from the direction of the Wafi mall via Oud Metha Road and Bu Kidra interchange near Nad Al Sheba racecourse. You'll need to circumvent the interchange and double back to a spot where you can safely pull off the road. You can also pull into the nature reserve off the Ras Al Khor Road as you approach Bu Kidra roundabout from Al Awir or Rashidiya. Look out for signs warning you not to approach the birds. Remember to take a pair of binoculars for close-up views.

The flamingos come to Dubai for the winter from lakes in northern Iran, and the government has tried to get them to breed here. The sanctuary also supports 30 percent of all wading birds found in the UAE. Indeed, Dubai has spent some of its oil wealth on environmental projects and has become something of a birdwatcher's paradise – there are up to 400 species in the country, around 90 of which are resident breeds. The UAE serves as a crossroads for north–south migrations from Europe to Africa and east–west migrations from India to the Near East. Up to 200 species, including bulbuls, doves, hoopoes, shrikes and wheatears, have been spotted at Emirates Golf Club alone, while in the city, Dubai Creek Golf & Yacht Club *(see Itinerary 2, page 34)* is home to parakeets, Indian rollers and little green bee-eaters.

Dubai's parks *(see Itinerary 6, page 46)* are also good places to spot birds. The best months for glimpsing migrating birds are October and March.

Right: a resident of the wildlife and waterbird sanctuary

8. DHOW CRUISE *(see map, p18–19)*

One of the best ways of enjoying the waterfront is to take an afternoon or evening *dhow* cruise.

If the sight of Dubai from the air is a treat, the view from the sea should be mandatory. The city has welcomed seafarers throughout its history and the deck of a boat still offers a fine platform from which to observe on-

shore activities. A Creek cruise or an afternoon's sailing along the Gulf coast places you at both the centre of city life and its periphery. Time seems to slow down on such a journey, giving the voyager a rare opportunity for observation and reflection in this hyperactive city. In this respect, taking to the water is not unlike venturing into the desert.

Although a short ride on an *abra* water taxi *(see Itinerary 1, page 26)* is not to be missed, it is the traditional wooden *dhow* that offers the most authentic type of Creek experience. On the Deira side of the Creek, you should be able to find a number of *dhows* that have been built or adapted for use by tourists between the Inter-Continental Hotel & Plaza and the Chamber of Commerce.

The Inter-Con's *Al Mansour Dhow* (tel: 04 222 7171) departs on cruises for dinner at 8.30pm. *Dhows* moored nearby that offer similar trips include those operated by Net Tours (tel: 04 266 6655), which operates daily dinner cruises from 7.30–10.30pm, but you are advised to book at least one day in advance to avoid disappointment.

On the opposite side of the Creek, near Al Garhoud Bridge, **Al Boom Tourist Village** (tel: 04 324 3000) is the biggest operator of *dhows* in Dubai. It runs day cruises on Fridays as well as nightly dinner cruises from 8.30pm. Alternatively, you might wish to consider chartering an *abra* from any of Dubai's four *abra* stations; this costs around Dhs 50 per hour.

Modern Alternatives

But just as the skyline has changed, so too have the boats. Modern alternatives to *dhows* and *abras* include the luxurious 34-metre (111-ft) *Danat Dubai*, run by Danat Dubai Cruises (tel: 04 351 1117), which offers lunch and dinner scenic cruises and charters from its Creek berth in Bur Dubai. Away from the Creek it offers truly fantastic views of the Arabian Gulf coast, covering the distance to Ajman, 24km (15 miles) away, in 1 hour and 35 minutes.

Above: everything is shipshape at the marina
Right: Sharjah Souk is a real treasure trove

9. SHARJAH SOUK *(see map, p50)*

Visit neighbouring Sharjah and find bargains in its huge modern souk.

To most of Dubai residents it's known simply as **Sharjah Souk** (Sat–Thur 9am–1pm and 4–10pm, closed Fri am), a treasure trove of carpets, antique furniture and Gulf mementos. But it's also called Sharjah New Souk, Blue Souk, Central Souk and Souk Al Markasi. The 'Five Dirham Souk' would be another appropriate moniker, not because it's known for its wonderful bargains – although there are some to be had if you're a shrewd haggler – but because it features on the UAE's five-dirham note.

Nothing in Dubai comes close to the souk in size, content or atmosphere. Some of the big shopping centres – City Centre in Deira and Bur Juman Centre in Bur Dubai – have air-conditioned shops that sell similar goods, but the choice isn't as wide as in the cramped, humid walkways of Sharjah Souk, whose vendors are more inclined to engage in the kind of bargaining that makes purchases so much more meaningful. Even Dubai's traditional old souks don't have the concentration of products available in Sharjah. Add the Jumeira set's opinion of the neighbouring emirate – it's seen as being a bit risqué – and you have the basis for an exciting and worthwhile shopping trip.

Sharjah Taxis

The best way to get there is by taxi (even the least knowledgeable Dubai cabbie should know the route). With a clear run the journey shouldn't take more than 20 minutes. However, many Sharjah residents work in Dubai and the Dubai-Sharjah highway becomes clogged with homeward-bound commuters between 6pm and 8pm. You'll probably need at least two hours to shop and will need to catch a Sharjah taxi back. These cabs aren't as clean and well-maintained as their Dubai counterparts, and they don't have meters, so agree the fare before you get in. You might want to rent a car, and/or combine a visit to the souk with sightseeing in Sharjah *(see Excursion 2, page 58).*

Situated between **Khalid Lagoon** and the green and pleasant **Al Ittihad Square** in the **Al Soor** district of the city, the souk itself consists of two long parallel buildings split by a road but joined by overhead walkways. The attractive exterior features blue tiles, decorative windows and large wind towers. The rounded roof has been likened to oil barrels lying side by side. Inside, the shops are on two levels. Unless you want perfume, cheap shoes, small electrical goods or audio tapes that are best found elsewhere, don't waste much time on the ground floor. The upstairs antique and carpet shops are particularly interesting and attract any number of souvenir-hunting visitors staying in other emirates. The first floor brings the description 'Aladdin's cave' to mind.

Cheap Restaurants

While in Sharjah you might want to take advantage of the relatively cheap restaurants. In 1985, Sharjah banned the sale of alcohol and, to offset a subsequent loss of business among Western expats, restaurateurs slashed their prices. Among a number of good possibilities is the pleasant **Dhow Restaurant**, a short walk from the souk. Other attractions of Sharjah include excursions across the lagoon and to the mouth of the Creek in *abra* water taxis and, on the opposite side of the flyover road by the souk, markets specialising in fish, and fruit and vegetables.

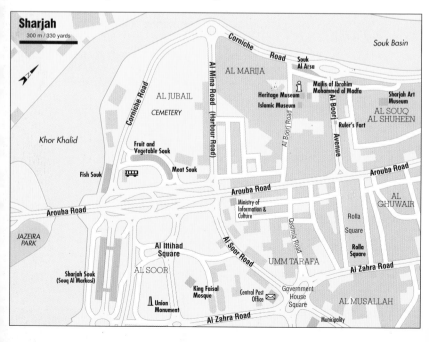

10. RACE NIGHT AT NAD AL SHEBA *(see map, p20–21)*

An evening at one of the most famous racecourses in the world.

The prospect of a night at the races on the edge of the Arabian desert is loaded with romantic possibilities, especially if you're prepared to pay the very reasonable day-member's fee at the **Nad Al Sheba Club** and watch the races from the balcony of the members' box high in the grandstand of **Nad Al Sheba**'s world-famous racecourse *(see Itinerary 3, page 36)*. But you don't have to dress up and experience corporate-style hospitality to enjoy

a night at Nad Al Sheba. Unlike most events in Dubai, admission is free throughout the November-April race season and with it comes unlimited access to most areas, including the lower portion of the grandstand and the area around the parade ring. Consequently, there's a unique multicultural atmosphere during each meeting, and it is being in the thick of this – rather than above it – that makes an evening at the races here so enjoyable.

The racecourse attracts the broad mixture of nationalities that comprises Dubai's population, with members of the East African communities, who love racing, particularly prominent. Walk around the floodlit venue between each of the evening's six or seven races and you'll have to pick your way through men, women and children sitting on blankets spread over the grass, playing cards, picnicking and generally making the evening a family outing.

Royal Attendance

Racing may no longer be the sport of European kings – Queen Elizabeth II notwithstanding – but it is emphatically the sport of Arab sheikhs and princes. And within those heady circles, not even such stellar figures as Saudi Arabia's Prince Khaled Abdullah, owner of the great 1986 champion racehorse Dancing Brave, can match the scale of influence now exerted over the Turf by Dubai's Maktoum family.

A race night at Nad Al Sheba offers you the best chance of seeing members of the ruling family up close. Sheikh Maktoum bin Rashid Al Maktoum, vice president of the UAE and ruler of Dubai, and his brother, General Sheikh Mohammed bin Rashid Al Maktoum, crown prince of Dubai and UAE minister of defence, attend when time permits. Sheikh Mohammed in par-

Above Left: a selection of 'hubble-bubble' pipes
Above: spectators at a Nad Al Sheba racenight

ticular is well-known to horse racing aficionados as the supremo behind the Godolphin stable. The royal box is in the centre of the grandstand.

The races begin at 7pm and are held every half hour thereafter. During the holy month of Ramadan, however, they begin at 9pm. If you fancy a flutter, the Pick Six competition offers a cash prize to anyone who guesses all six of the winning horses, thereby cleverly generating a vested interest at an event where gambling per se is illegal. The Pick Six forms are available on entry and are as simple to complete as a lottery form; they must be submitted at least 15 minutes before the first race.

If you happen to be in Dubai during the last week of March, pay the entrance fee to a day at the **Dubai World Cup**. This, the highlight of Dubai's social calendar, attracts crowds of 35,000, often including celebrity race fans such as Imran Khan, Rod Stewart and Bo Derek. With prize money of US$15 million, it's the richest horse race in the world.

11. MOSQUE VISIT AND CULTURAL LUNCH
(see map, p20–21)

Sample a taste of local life by joining an expedition organised by the Sheikh Mohammed Centre for Cultural Understanding.

About 75 percent of the UAE's population of over four million are expatriates, so it's quite possible to visit Dubai and leave without having met a single UAE national or indeed a Gulf Arab (excluding airport and post office workers). But you're bound to meet locals if you visit the worthy **Sheikh Mohammed Centre for Cultural Understanding** (tel: 04 353 6666). Established by and named after Dubai's crown prince, and based in the Bas-

takia district of Bur Dubai (Sat–Wed 9am–2pm, Thur 11.30am– 2pm) the centre aims to promote mutual understanding and acceptance among people from different cultures. Its guided tours of the beautiful Jumeira Mosque, run 10–11.30am on Sunday and Thursday, are currently the only way for non-Muslims to enter the building. Visitors are invited to meet at the mosque and should be dressed appropriately, with arms and legs covered (plus headscarves for women). No booking is required.

In its bid to support 'free exchanges of ideas about Dubai, its people and its culture', the Sheikh Mohammed Centre also organises cultural lunches at the centre, providing insights into a culture that is usually poorly represented in the Western media, and a holiday experience that's sure to be enriching.

Left: inside Jumeira Mosque
Right: baby sharks at Deira fish souk

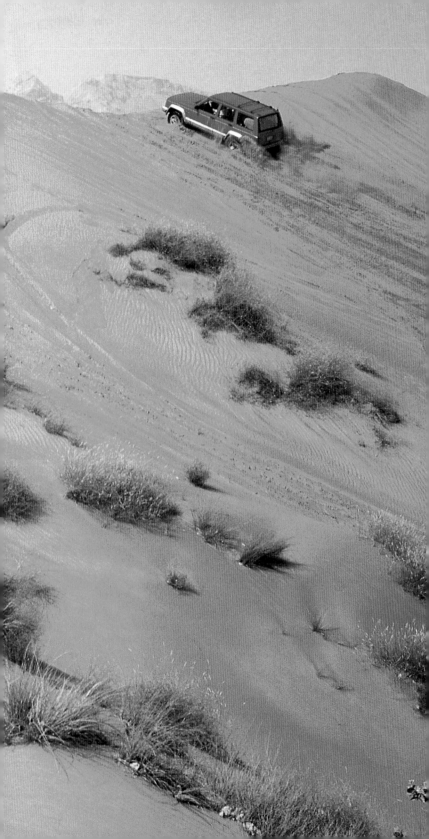

Excursions

1. DESERT ADVENTURE *(see map, p56)*

A visit to Dubai isn't complete without a trip into the desert. For most people this is best done through an official tour company.

Forget the Creek, forget the beaches, forget the shopping: if you haven't spent at least a few hours in the desert you haven't truly experienced Dubai. For all its striking modernity, Dubai is built on sand and the desert way of life, and explorations of the dunes and wadis in the outlying emirate will help you better understand the city and its people. If that seems too worthy a reason, the desert can be stunningly beautiful and tremendous fun – speeding over the dunes in a luxury 4X4 with an expert driver is thoroughly exhilarating. In this case, the 'experience of a lifetime' cliché rings true.

Some 65 percent of the UAE's 85,000 sq km (33,000 sq miles) is desert. The term encompasses a variety of landscapes and conditions: as well as the rolling dunes of *Lawrence of Arabia* fame, it includes salt flats *(sabkha)*, flood plains, mountains and river valleys. The desert that begins on the outskirts of Dubai (or more accurately within the city limits, where every vacant lot is sandy) forms part of the Saharo-Arabian Desert, the most extensive dry zone in the world. It's possible to enter it in **Al Awir**, near Dubai Country Club, and to see nothing but desert until you tap the sand from your shoes on the Syria-Lebanon border thousands of kilometres away.

The Largest Dunes

You don't need to travel so far to gauge the desert's vastness. The nearest large dunes to Dubai are found at **Qarn Nazwa** on the Dubai-Hatta road, beginning about 15 km (9 miles) beyond Lahbab roundabout. These dunes offer a glimpse of the stereotypical desert landscape, and you don't have to join a specialist tour to see them. Be aware that this is a popular area for dune driving, so if you're craving solitude and silence, you may be disappointed.

Heading inland from Dubai's coastal beaches towards Qarn Nazwa, you first pass through terrain known as *sabkha* – formed over the course of 7,000 years by wind erosion and tides – followed by a landscape of scrubby sand. (You might be surprised by the desert's greenness; residents say it's becoming greener by the year.) You then encounter barren rolling dunes tinted red by deposits of iron oxide; run the sand through your fingers and it seems to be mixed with paprika.

Don't even think about venturing further off-road in a rental 4X4 unless you're with a local expert and a second vehicle.

Left: a roller-coaster journey
Right: camel country

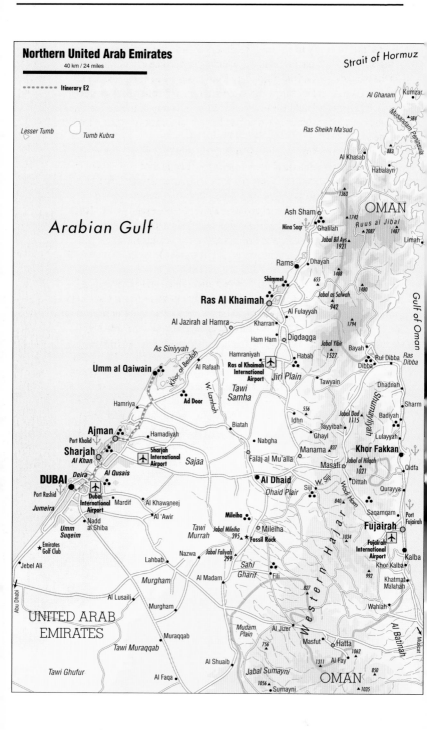

Northern United Arab Emirates

40 km / 24 miles

⸱⸱⸱⸱⸱⸱⸱⸱ Itinerary E2

Strait of Hormuz

Arabian Gulf

Al Ghanam · Kumzar

Lesser Tumb · *Tumb Kubra*

Ras Sheikh Ma'sud

584

Mussandam Peninsula

Al Khasab

Habalayn

OMAN

1363

Ash Sham

Mina Saqr · Ghalilah

1742

Ruus al Jibal

2087 1487

Limah

Jabal Bil Ays 1921

Rams · Dhayah

Shimmel

1488

655

Ras Al Khaimah

Al Fulayyah

Jabal as Salwah 942

1480

Gulf of Oman

Al Jazirah al Hamra

Kharran

Ham Ham · **Digdagga**

1794

Ras Dibba

As Siniyyah

Al Rafaah

Hamraniyah

Ras al Khaimah International Airport

Jiri Plain

Habab

Jabal Yibir 1527

Bayah

Ruł Dibba

Dibba

Dhadnah

Umm al Qaiwain

Khor al Beidah

W. Lamhah

Tawi Samha

Tawyain

Shumailiyah

Sharm

Hamriya

Ad Door

556

Jabal Dad 1115

Badiyah

Biatah

Idhn

Tayyibah

Lulayyah

Ajman

Port Khalid

Hamadiyah

Nabgha

Ghayl

Manama 837

Khor Fakkan

Sharjah

Al Khan

Sharjah International Airport

Sajaa

Falaj al Mu'alla

Masafi

Jabal al Hilqah 1021

Qidfa

DUBAI

Deira

Al Qusais

Al Dhaid

Siji · *W. Siji*

Dittah

Port Rashid

Ohaid Plair

840

Wadi Ham

Qurayya

Jumeira

Dubai International Airport

Mardif

Al Khawaneej

Al 'Awir

Mileiha

Saqamqam

Port Fujairah

Umm Suqeim

Nadd al Shiba

Tawi Murrah

Jabal Mileiha 395

Mileiha

★ **Fossil Rock**

1034

Fujairah

Fujairah International Airport

★ *Emirates Golf Club*

Lahbab

Nazwa

Jabal Faliyah 299

992

Kalba

· Jebel Ali

Sahl Gharif

Fili

Khor Kalba

Western Hajar

Al Madam

827

Khatmat Malahah

Murgham

Al Lusaili

UNITED ARAB EMIRATES

Murgham

Al Batinah

Wahlah

Murqaqab

Mudam Plain

Al Jizer

756

Masfut

Hatta

1062

Tawi Muraqqab

Al Shuaib

1311 · Al Fay

850

Tawi Ghufur·

Al Faqa

Jabal Sumayni

OMAN

1056 · Surnayni

1035

Right: a ringside seat

By far the best way to explore the desert is with one of the numerous specialist tour companies, many of which have become established only in the past few years. Itineraries vary from company to company, but all tend to include camel farms, Bedouin villages and roller-coaster dune rides. Your guide should fill you in on the Bedouin way of life and desert ecology, as well as identifying plants and any animal tracks you might find in the sand.

Arabian Adventures (tel: 04 303 4888; www.arabian-adventures.com), Net Tours (tel: 04 266 6655) and Orient Tours (tel: 06 568 2323; www. orienttours.ae) are among several well established companies offering half- or full-day forays into the desert. Your hotel should have information on specialist tours, and may even run its own programme. For example, the Hatta Fort Hotel *(see Excursion 3, page 63)* has an excellent tour to **Fossil Rock**, so called because of the marine-life fossils that can be seen there.

Fossil Rock and Big Red

If possible, opt for a tour that visits dunes *and* wadis, ideally Fossil Rock and Big Red, both of which are justifiably popular with the locals. Another favourite is **Wadih Bih** – further afield but manageable in a day trip that describes a rugged route from **Ras Al Khaimah** through the canyons, gorges and terraced hillsides of the 1,200-m (4,000-ft) **Hajar Mountains**.

The best time to experience the desert is late afternoon, when the light is as soft and warm as the sand underfoot. You might opt for a desert dinner tour (4–10pm), during which you'll see sunset and a night sky that, away from any ambient light, is remarkably clear. Alternatively, if you take a 24-hour overnight trip, departing Dubai at 3pm, you'll see sunset and, after a night watching shooting stars, sunrise. If you're prepared to forego the comfort of a luxury 4X4 in your search for excitement, contact Desert Rangers (tel: 04 340 2408; www.desertrangers.com), which organises activities such as sandboarding and dune-buggy Safaris.

2. THE NORTHERN EMIRATES *(see map, p56)*

The drive from Dubai through the northern emirates of Sharjah, Ajman and Umm Al Qaiwain is like a journey back in time: the further you travel, the more you can envisage how Dubai looked before the oil boom.

The northern emirates extend to Ras Al Khaimah, 96km (60 miles) from Dubai, but with so much to see and do, this car-based day trip ends in **Umm Al Qaiwain**. As you head northeast, away from Dubai, you pass through a less wealthy, less populous and less developed UAE. At Umm Al Qaiwain (population 41,000), you might feel as though you've travelled back in time to the pre-oil days, when Sheikh Saeed lived in a modest house on Dubai Creek and the coastal emirates were known as the Trucial States. You could spend a day or more in any one of the emirates mentioned here – what follows is less of a one-day itinerary than an overview of the route with suggestions. If you leave Dubai at 9am and allow for three hours in Sharjah, an hour or so in Ajman and two and a half hours in Umm Al Qaiwain, you should have a fascinating day packed with very varied experiences.

The road to **Sharjah**, the UAE's third largest emirate after Abu Dhabi and Dubai, is well-signposted, but once you're there it's very easy to get lost on streets that can be even more congested and chaotic than Dubai's. The best way to avoid the traffic is to bypass what appears to be the most direct route into the city along the Dubai-Sharjah highway. Come off the highway either immediately after Interchange 1 –

Above: view from Sharjah bridge
Left: King Faisal Mosque

following a road that skirts three lagoons and enters the city as Arouba Road at a new and impressive large mosque – or just before the highway rises into a flyover. For the second option, head left at the roundabout underneath the flyover in the direction of the same impressive mosque, at which you should turn right.

A Cultural Capital

Arouba Road is the most attractive entrance to a city that was named cultural capital of the Arab world by UNESCO in 1998. (Until alcohol was banned here in 1985, it had a more promising future as a tourist destination than Dubai). As the road rises to cross Sharjah's Khalid Creek at Sharjah Bridge you can see Port Khalid – the towering metal frames are oil rigs due for repairs – and fishing *dhows* clustered around the fish souk. To the right, the 10 sq km (4 sq mile) Jazeira Park occupies its own island. Beyond this, the 100-m (330-ft) high fountain at Khalid Lagoon is the third highest in the world, after those in Geneva and Jeddah. A little further on, Sharjah Souk *(see Itinerary 9, page 49)* can be seen on the right, along with the gold-topped Al Ittihad ('Union') Monument and the enormous King Faisal Mosque, which towers over the verdant Al Ittihad Square.

Beyond a man-made grassy knoll with a flower-bed urging passers-by to 'Smile, You Are In Sharjah', you can see **King Abd Al Aziz Street** leading towards newer neighbourhoods. Until 1976, this street formed the main runway of the UAE's first airport. Originally established in 1932 as a stopover for British Imperial Airways flights from London to Australia, the airport was also an RAF base and home to the Trucial Oman Scouts. The UAE's first hotel, the Fortress Hotel just off King Abd Al Aziz Street, has been restored and, with an air traffic control tower, forms a small aviation museum.

Take the right slip road immediately after Sharjah Bridge. If you want to visit the Sharjah Souk or the aviation museum, carefully cross several lanes of traffic towards a road that cuts through the park and navigate your way from there. Otherwise, continue as far as you can after the slip road, follow the road left underneath a flyover and then turn right onto Al Mina Road. You're on the right road if Sharjah Cinema is immediately to your right. The bird and animal souk, where falcons are sold, is in a parallel street to the left.

Continue to a small roundabout at the Creek and turn right onto Corniche Road, along one side of which are moored numerous *dhows*. You'll continue along this road towards Ajman later, but first

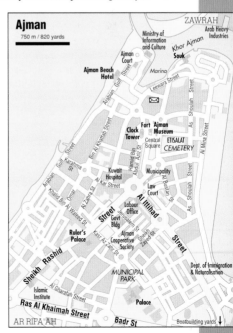

park the car and take time to explore the heritage areas that have been restored on either side of **Al Boorj Avenue** (aka Bank Street): they convey a sense of life in the days when Sharjah was a more important Gulf trading centre than Dubai.

The Oldest Souk

Souk Al Arsa (Sat–Thur 9am–1pm and 4.30–9pm, Fri 4.30–9pm), the UAE's oldest souk, is set a little off Corniche Road before Bank Street in an enchanting neighbourhood of alleyways, minarets and wind-towers. Built with coral, limestone and plaster, and shaded by a palm-frond roof, the souk is full of delightful antiques shops and stalls that sell everything from handicrafts

and trinkets to honey and tobacco. Its friendly coffee shop is popular with elderly locals.

There are several museums in the area, including: **Sharjah Heritage Museum** (Tues–Thur, Sat, Sun 9am–1pm and 5–8 pm, Fri 5–8pm) in the former home of the Al Naboodah trading family; **Sharjah Islamic Museum** (Tues–Thur, Sat, Sun 9am–1pm and 5–8pm, Fri 5–8pm; www.uaeinteract.com/culture), in the former residence of one Said bin Mohammed Al Shamsi; and the **Majlis of Ibrahim Mohammed Al Madfa** (Sat–Thur 9am–1pm and 5–8pm, Fri 5–8pm), founder of the region's first newspaper in 1927 and at one time an adviser to the ruling Al Qasimi family. The majlis' distinctive round wind-tower is the only one of its kind in the UAE.

The **Ruler's Fort** (Tues–Thur, Sat, Sun 9am–1pm and 5–8 pm, Fri 5–8pm) is in the middle of Bank Street, standing on what is now a large traffic island in a small canyon of banks and offices. Another heritage area, which includes the purpose-built **Sharjah Art Museum** (Tues–Thur, Sat, Sun 9am–1pm and 5–8pm, Fri 5–8pm) and the venerable **Ad Dalil Mosque**, fronts onto the Corniche Road on the other side of Bank Street.

Back in your car, continue past the large Holiday Inn hotel and along a quite regal avenue of palm trees, wrought-iron railings and, most noticeable, a showcase fountain that indicates that the Ruler's Palace is on your left. At each of a succession of small roundabouts, bear left, and keep hugging the coast road. With its pristine, white-sand beach, this area is like a less developed version of Dubai's Jumeira coastline. You're now passing through the Sharjah suburbs into Ajman.

The Smallest Emirate

In terms of ambience, **Ajman** is much like the Dubai of the 1970s. The smallest of the UAE's seven emirates (with a population of only 160,000), Ajman has no oil wealth and still relies on traditional industries such as ship repairs, fish-

Above: a family stroll past Sharjah's Ad Dalil Mosque
Right: Ajman Museum

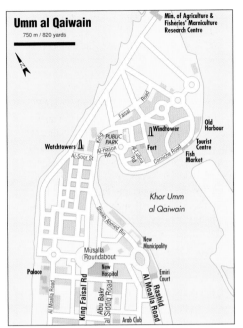

Umm al Qaiwain

750 m / 820 yards

Min. of Agriculture & Fisheries' Marniculture Research Centre

Watchtowers

Al-Soor St

PUBLIC PARK

Al-Hason Rd

King Faisal Road

Al-Ithia Rd

Windtower

Fort

Corniche Road

Old Harbour

Tourist Centre

Fish Market

Khor Umm al Qaiwain

Sheikh Ahmed Bin

Musalla Roundabout

Palace

Al Moala Road

King Faisal Rd

New Hospital

Abu Bakr al Siddiq Road

New Municipality

Rashid Al Moala Road

Emiri Court

Arab Club

ing and *dhow*-building. Its main attraction is the excellent **Ajman Museum** (Sun–Thur 9am–1pm and 4–7pm, Fri 4–7pm) in the town's old fort. To reach the museum, take a right turn at the Ajman Beach Hotel and follow the road alongside the edge of the pretty marina to Leewara Street. Turn right and, at the first roundabout, bear left towards Clocktower roundabout and Central Square. The fort will be to your left. Built in around 1775, the fort was the ruler's official residence until 1970 and Ajman's police station in the 1970s. More appealing in some ways than its Dubai equivalent – the quieter, almost rustic setting helps – the museum has a fine example of a wind-tower which, unlike those in some other UAE museums, is fully functioning.

Umm Al Qaiwain

To continue to Umm Al Qaiwain, pass through Ajman along Hamid Bin Abdul Aziz Street. At the first roundabout head for Al Ittihad Street at your eleven o'clock. Continue until this street joins Badr Street and turn left. You're now on the road to Umm Al Qaiwain. If in doubt, follow signs for Ras Al Khaimah. The road from Ajman to Umm Al Qaiwain passes through the first *sabkha* desert since leaving Dubai. **Umm Al Qaiwain** basks on its own head-

land well off the main road linking Dubai with Ras Al Khaimah. It's about halfway between the two and is well-signposted.

The old town is built on little more than a sandy spit at the tip of the headland. Approaching it along King Faisal Road, you might not realise that you're actually passing through the heart of the modern capital of an emirate, albeit the UAE's second-smallest. Umm Al Qaiwain is so quiet that it's quite possible you won't see anyone on the streets until you reach the old town, and even then you're likely to see more goats than people. Other than the occasional Mercedes and BMW, the odd battered old Land Rover or antiquated Indian Padmini, the roads are virtually free of traffic. Three ancient **watchtowers**, once part of a fortified defensive wall, mark the boundary of the old town at the narrowest part of the headland, where King Faisal Road meets Al Soor Street. At this point you'll see the old town away to your right across a an enormous lagoon. On part of the lagoon's shoreline you will find Umm Al Qaiwain's most appealing attraction – mangrove trees.

Take the first right and follow the road past a small public park. The town's old **fortress** – which, much like the one in Ajman, served as the residence of the local ruler in the years before it became a police station – stands in a small square beyond the roundabout ahead. Take a right at the roundabout and follow Corniche Road past the fish market, where you're likely to see fishermen mending broken nets. Just before the road arcs left to continue its loop through the old town (before rejoining King Faisal Road), turn right into the **Umm Al Qaiwain tourist centre** (tel: 06 765 0000). Park the car and continue your exploration of the area by boat, which you can hire here by booking in advance.

Hiring a Boat

The criteria for choosing a type of boat to rent depends entirely on how you want the afternoon to pan out. A speedboat – and even jet skis – are tremen-

Above: mother and child at a Sharjah souk

dously exciting but aren't much use if you're hoping to spot some wildlife. Conversely, a catamaran is a wonderful way to relax while exploring **As Siniyyah** and the other, smaller islands that dot Umm Al Qaiwain's sheltered lagoon. You might, however, find the seamanship involved somewhat intimidating, in which case a motorboat is an excellent compromise. Unlike the speedboat option, which gives you a member of the centre's staff at the helm, you'll have the motorboat to yourself, so if you spot any wildlife – this is the habitat of herons, cormorants, flamingos, turtles and even dugong (sea cows) – you can always cut the engine and drift.

The boats are inexpensive and available to hire by the half hour or hour. The experience can be followed at sunset by refreshments from the centre's licensed bar. Allow an hour for the 40-km (25-mile) return journey to Dubai.

3. HATTA *(see map, p56)*

This is a day (or two-day) trip into the Hajar Mountains to Hatta, with its fort and springs. Avoid going on Fridays and public holidays, when the track to Hatta Pools is clogged with 4X4s, trucks and even saloon cars from the city.

To do Hatta justice you need to set aside a whole day, at least. To make the most of this trip, you might consider spending the night at the excellent Hatta Fort Hotel (tel: 04 852 3211) – an enchanting oasis surrounded by dry, jagged, volcanic rock.

The pretty fortress village of **Hatta**, in the foothills of the Hajar Mountains, is a popular weekend retreat with both UAE nationals and expats seeking to escape the heat and humidity of the Gulf coast. But it's not just its favourable climate and slow pace of life that make Hatta an appealing destination: its heritage and landscape make the hour-long drive from Dubai worthwhile. A large dam ensures a constant water supply, and the altitude enables farm crops to flourish. The approach to Hatta emphasises the remarkable contrasts in habitat: beautiful beaches and open desert country give way to rocky mountain ranges.

To get to Hatta from Dubai, follow signs for Al Awir, Hatta and Oman from the Bu Kidra interchange near Nad Al Sheba racecourse. Not long after setting off you'll see the flare from a Margham oilfield stack to the

Right: Hatta Fort Hotel

right. About halfway into the journey you pass the Qarn Nazwa dunes *(see Excursion 1, page 55)*. After the roundabout at Madam, the dunes flatten into the gravel Madam Plain and scrub terrain reminiscent of parts of Africa. Watch out for camels on the road, especially at night.

For much of this section of the journey you will be in Omani territory on what, some 90 million years ago, was the seabed. It is interesting to note that Hatta is surrounded by territory belonging to Oman, Ras al-Khaimah and Ajman. Visitors don't need visas or passports to enter territory that became an anomaly when the borders were drawn up. The borderpost for Oman is about 5km (3 miles) east of Hatta. The first sign to confirm that you are nearing Hatta is the sight of roadside carpet stalls, followed by the appearance of hilltop summer homes that belong to Dubai's sheikhs and wealthy businessmen. When you reach the roundabout with an open-sided fortress in the middle, either turn left for the leafy gateway to the Hatta Fort Hotel, or turn right for Hatta Heritage Village and the road to Hatta Pools.

Hatta Heritage Village (Sat–Thur 8.30am–8.30pm, Fri 3pm–8.30pm) is a re-creation of a traditional mountain village that illustrates the community's colourful history – the first fort in the emirate of Dubai was built here in 1790. Check out the fascinating variety of mud and *barasti* (palm frond) houses, and a restored *falaj* irrigation system that channels water through the village to the neighbourhood's date-palm gardens. The watchtower that looms high over the village dates back to 1850.

Hatta Pools

The main attractions at Hatta are the **Hatta Pools** and the off-road drive that continues beyond the pools through Wadi Qahfi to the Omani village of Rayy. The dirt track which leads to the pools begins several kilometres from Hatta itself. The Hatta Fort Hotel is happy to provide navigation sheets with directions, distance markers and key landmarks to guests who have their own 4X4s. Alternatively, you might book a 4X4 tour with the hotel to share the expense of vehicle and driver. Don't expect idyllic pools, cascading waterfalls and a brimming river at Hatta Pools and you won't be disappointed. The parched but stunning landscape around the pools bears comparison with the surface of the moon. The access track is dusty, the riverbed largely dry, while the spring pools are made up of low-level, slow-moving water. Throughout the year, there's enough water at crossing points to make a splash.

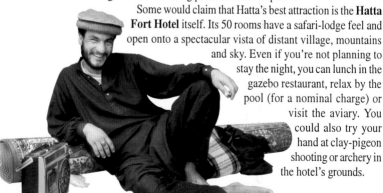

Some would claim that Hatta's best attraction is the **Hatta Fort Hotel** itself. Its 50 rooms have a safari-lodge feel and open onto a spectacular vista of distant village, mountains and sky. Even if you're not planning to stay the night, you can lunch in the gazebo restaurant, relax by the pool (for a nominal charge) or visit the aviary. You could also try your hand at clay-pigeon shooting or archery in the hotel's grounds.

Left: selling carpets

4. DIBBA AND THE ARABIAN SEA *(see map, p56)*

A journey east to the craggy coast at Dibba by the Musandam Peninsula.

After a while you might find that Dubai's beaches, for all their beauty, can begin to feel monotonous. The land is virtually flat and very little of the coastline retains the wildness of the desert interior. If you decide that it's time to sunbathe on a different kind of beach, a day trip to **Dibba** is highly recommended. The beach at Dibba is wilder, more isolated, untouched by tourism, and is framed on three sides by rugged mountains.

Dibba, nestled below the Musandam Peninsula that divides the Arabian Gulf from the Arabian Sea and Indian Ocean, shares its coastline with Oman. In fact, the Dibba Bayah neighbourhood of Dibba is actually within Oman's territory – a somewhat strange arrangement involving a bubble of land that guards the Strait of Hormuz. The remainder of the coastal town is administered by the emirates of Fujairah (Dibba Muhallab) and Sharjah (Dibba Al Hisn). It's Omani Dibba we're heading for, but, as was the case on the road to Hatta, you don't need to worry about border formalities as there aren't any.

Desert Park

From Dubai, you should allow for a two-hour car journey. There are two choices of route: you can either head north to Sharjah, initially following signs to Sharjah International Airport, or take a newer, quicker road past Dubai International Airport and Rashidiya. Either way, at Junction 8 of the Sharjah-Al Dhaid road you pass **Sharjah Natural History Museum and Desert Park** (Sat, Mon–Wed 9am–7pm, Thur noon–7pm, Fri 2–10pm; www.shj-museum.gov.ae). The park, set up in 1995, is a breeding ground for rare Arabian leopards, foxes, ibex, oryx and gazelles. At Al Dhaid, a small oasis

Above: Friday drumming near Dibba

town kept green by an ancient network of underground *falaj* channels that run from the mountains, to Sharjah, follow the signs to Masafi and Fujairah.

The scenery starts to change from plains to mountains. In a small gorge about 5km (3 miles) before Masafi you'll pass through the **Friday Market** (open all week despite its name), where you can buy refreshments and souvenirs. Local specialities include inexpensive ornamental pots, many for holding candles, with patterns cut into the sides. These make wonderful home decorations but be warned that they are extremely fragile. You can also get good deals on machine-made carpets.

At Masafi, which is home to a popular UAE brand of bottled water, turn left around a large roundabout towards Dibba. From here the road rises and falls through striking scenery before entering the town. On Dibba's outskirts, turn left at Dolphin roundabout, go straight through Tower roundabout and turn right at the small Sharjah police box. This road takes you to Dibba Al Hisn's picturesque seafront, where you'll have a great view of the sweep of the bay and the mountains on either side.

Marooned Fish

Continuing along the corniche with the Arabian Sea on your right, you will soon pass a sign marking the border with Oman. After driving straight through a small roundabout and an area with roadside flood markers, turn right onto a stony track that heads towards a cliff. This is where you might notice thousands of fish marooned some distance from the sea – they're sardines that the fishermen have left to dry before they are processed into fertiliser. When you've gone as far as you can on the track, park the car and the beach will be over the sandy rise to your right.

The chances are that you'll have **Dibba beach** almost to yourself, though you might be confronted by curious villagers. If it's a public holiday, however, you could well be joined by hordes of holidaymakers from the north-

ern Emirates and Dubai. There are no shops for several kilometres, so be sure to bring all the food and water you might need. A few palm frond-topped shelters on the beach provide shade.

Look out for the ruins of a small settlement, though it can be difficult to delineate because its stone walls are set against the cliffs at the top of the beach. The ruins hint at a rich history: in 633 the Muslim forces of Caliph Abu Baker waged a great battle to suppress a local rebellion and reclaim the Arabian peninsula for Islam. You can see the enormous cemetery that contains some 10,000 headstones of those who lost their lives in the battle.

Left: snorkelling at Sandy Beach
Right: Masafi road from Dibba

Leisure Activities

SHOPPING

To a large proportion of visitors, Dubai's assorted attractions – from the cultural to the rest-and-recreation variety – are mere sideshows or time-fillers to be enjoyed between visits to the main event: the shops. For dedicated shoppers, male and female, Dubai is simply heavenly. An amazing array of goods suit diverse budgets and tastes, and many items are tax-free.

In recognition of the city's popularity with shoppers, the municipal authorities established an annual month-long extravaganza, the Dubai Shopping Festival (DSF) in 1996. Thus every January there's a carnival atmosphere and a large number of tourist-oriented spin-off activities. It's a tribute to the success of DSF that a second festival, Dubai Summer Surprises (DSS), has been added to the calendar. This has enlivened the city during the quieter (hotter) months between June and September. Of course the world-renowned Dubai Duty Free is open throughout the year.

Don't be fooled into believing that every item available for purchase in Dubai is cheaper than you'll find elsewhere in the world. Dubai's shops may have become the stuff of lore, but this owes as much to canny marketing as reality. Although extremely good deals are to be had on everything from jewellery to computers during DSFs – when prices in participating outlets are driven down by the government – visiting shopaholics will literally pay a heavy price if they forget to calculate the price of goods according to the exchange rate, assume that everything is a bargain and blithely put all purchases on the credit card.

One way to attempt to get a good deal is, of course, to bargain. This is virtually obligatory in traditional souks but less common in modern malls, though even there it's worth asking for 'the best price'. In the souks you're more likely to get a larger discount with cash, as opposed to plastic or travellers' cheques. The trick is initially to disguise your interest in the item that you really want, and then to nonchalantly offer half for it. How far upwards you negotiate from there depends on your cunning and the seller's guile.

So, when shopping in Dubai, it's up to you to be judicious, to bargain hard to get the best price and, as some visitors forget to their cost, make sure you've left plenty of room for your purchases in your luggage. Given Dubai's eclectic combination of ethnic wares, designer labels and household-name brands, it's very easy to buy too much and then be unable to transport it all home.

Generally, the best time to shop is in the morning or late afternoon/evening. Many shops and souks close in the early afternoon and on Friday mornings. Most malls are open until 10pm, some later during holidays and the holy month of Ramadan. If possible, stay away from shops in out-of-town hotels, which tend to be the expensive option of last-minute, panic buyers.

Traditional Souks

For good deals and a vibrant atmosphere, nothing beats Dubai's traditional souks, the most famous of which is Deira's dazzling gold souk (9.30am–1pm, 2–10pm, Fri 4–10pm), from which Dubai acquired the nickname 'City of Gold'. Prices here are linked to the international daily gold rate.

For more information on this and other souks, see the *Itineraries* section. You'll find

Left: electronic goods arrive by *dhow*
Right: shopping at the gold souk

more details on the gold souk in *Itinerary 2 (see page 31)*. Sharjah souk is also included in the *Itineraries* section *(see page 49)*. After Deira Tower mall in Al Nasr Square, Sharjah souk is probably the best place to buy carpets from countries such as Iran, Pakistan and China. The souk also has a wide selection of 'antiques', such as coffee pots and decorative *khanjar* daggers – short curved knives traditionally worn tucked into the waists of men in the region.

Shopping Areas

As opposed to souks in the traditional sense, there are areas of Dubai where the shops specialise in particular goods. For brand-name electronic goods, try Al Faheidi Road in Bur Dubai or the area around Al Nasr Square in Deira. The port end of Khalid Ibn Al Waleed Road (Bank Street) in Bur Dubai is the place for computers and software. If you want colourful silks or textiles, check out the many small shops in the streets to the rear of Dubai Museum in Bur Dubai, while cheap clothes shops and tailors can be found in Karama. You can buy local artwork at the Majlis Gallery *(See Itinerary 1, page 27)* or the Creative Art Centre, Jumeira (tel: 344 4394).

Dubai has a small number of high streets. Deira's Al Riqqa Road, a pleasant tree-lined avenue of boutiques, is sometimes called the Champs Elysées of Dubai. The parallel Maktoum Road's boutiques include those of Gianni Versace, Dolce & Gabbana and, in the Majestic Centre, Cartier. In Satwa, on the Bur Dubai side of the Creek, there are a variety of boutiques in Al Dhiyafah Road *(See Itinerary 3, page 39)*.

The Malls

For air-conditioned comfort and convenient access, nothing beats Dubai's malls. Most have numerous gold and jewellery stores that might interest you in the unlikely event that the gold souk doesn't meet your requirements. **Al Ghurair City** on Al Riqqa Road is the granddaddy of them all, with some 400 stores, including Giordano, Benetton and a carpet shop.

The people's mall is undoubtedly **Deira City Centre**. If you're self-catering, this is the place to come to buy provisions – the fare at its huge Carrefour hypermarket will supplement whatever's available at the various Spinneys supermarkets dotted around the city. Note that alcohol can be bought only at specific outlets, and even then you must have a permit. Deira City Centre's stores also include Damas Jewellery, Burberrys, The Body Shop, Next, Debenhams, Woolworths as well as an area specialising in local products such as textiles, carpets and antiques.

On the other side of the Creek, next to the stunning Pyramids bar, restaurant and spa complex on Garhoud Bridge Road, the **Wafi** shopping mall is recognisable by its glass pyramid-shaped top. Here you can buy clothing from Chanel, Tag Heuer and Nike among others. The nearby **Lamcy Plaza** is a little more down-market but has a remarkable replica of Tower Bridge in its atrium. In Bur Dubai, the stately **Bur Juman Centre** on Trade Centre Road is home to several luxury fashion stores, including Christian Dior, Polo Ralph Lauren and DKNY, while its Grand Stores outlet specialises in Nikon cameras.

In Jumeira, the Italian-style **Mercato Mall** has brand-name fashion shops and also a Virgin Megastore.

Bookshops

If you are looking for information on this part of the world, your best bets are Magrudy's bookshops in Magrudy's Mall, Jumeira, Deira City Centre or the Bur Juman Centre. Along with the popular Book Corner, Books Plus and Dar al Hikma, Magrudy's has a wider selection of volumes on Dubai and the UAE than you are likely to find anywhere else in the world.

Left: Deira City Centre Mall

EATING OUT

If Dubai's shops promote the idea of excess baggage, then its fabulous restaurants are likely to induce thoughts of doggy bags. For dedicated diners, whether carnivorous or vegetarian, Dubai is the proverbial paradise. Restaurants here offer a wide choice of meals at a variety of prices, and virtually all tastes are catered for.

The quality of food in Dubai is something of a secret. Whereas the city is renowned for its shopping, it's not much recognised for its culinary successes. There isn't any Dubai Eating Festival to complement the internationally-marketed shopping equivalent, though such an event is not beyond the realms of possibility. Certainly all the ingredients are here, from roadside vendors selling cheap but delicious *schwarmas* (meat cooked on a vertical spit, then sliced, topped with tahini and salad and served in pitta bread) to the most elegant fine dining in the luxury hotels.

In the main, for Arabic food read Lebanese. *Mezze*, small dishes and dips, are the region's equivalent of tapas. Staple *mezze* scooped up with flat Arabic bread are: houmous (a chickpea paste with olive oil, garlic and lemon juice); *tabbouleh* (a herb salad with bulgar wheat); *fattoush* (a finely chopped tomato, cucumber and lettuce salad); *mutabel* (similar to houmous but made with eggplant); and felafel (fried chickpea patties). *Mezze* are often followed by a main course but can be eaten as satisfying meals in themselves.

Emirati food, such as it exists as a separate cuisine, derives from simple Bedouin fare and consists mainly of fish, chicken and lamb, served as kebabs or biriani-style with rice. Common flavourings include cumin, cardamom and coriander. Al Areesh, at Al Boom Tourist Village (tel: 04 324 3000) near Al Garhoud Bridge is Dubai's closest approximation to a true Emirati restaurant.

Puddings often include nuts, syrup and fresh cream, and to end the meal you will usually be offered Arabic coffee or mint tea.

Many of Dubai's restaurants are located in hotels, but don't let that put you off. The hotels here are vibrant social centres for nationals and expatriates alike. Those that have a number of different food outlets look and feel like mini-neighbourhoods through which you can stroll in air-conditioned comfort. And, in contrast to the majority of 'high street' restaurants, hotels are licensed to sell alcohol. They will also accept all major credit cards, unlike the many small establishments that require cash.

Cultural Considerations

It's worth familiarising yourself with a few important cultural points:

Firstly, whatever your religion, it is illegal to eat in public in daylight during the holy month of Ramadan, when Muslims abstain from food and drink from sunrise until sunset. Hotel and club restaurants do open during Ramadan but their eating areas are screened so as not to offend Muslim sensibilities. But you shouldn't let Ramadan dissuade you from visiting the city. On the contrary, if you go to a Ramadan tent in the evening – and you would be most welcome – the bonhomie and feasting that you experience could prove to be one of the highlights of your stay.

Secondly, although pork and alcohol are not consumed by Muslims, most restaurants use them as ingredients in dishes prepared for foreigners. Dishes that incorporate these ingredients are usually highlighted on menus.

Thirdly, locals tend to dine late at night, so if you want to enjoy a good atmosphere

Above: a Boardwalk bar in the glowing light of dusk

while eating, plan dinner from around 9pm and, if possible, book ahead.

The following recommendations have not been chosen for quality alone (though most are exceptional) but also for ambience and considerations of budget and location. If you find yourself hungry for more, you could consult *Dubai Explorer*, available at bookshops and large supermarkets.

Regional

Al Khayal
Jumeirah Beach Hotel, Jumeira
Tel: 04 406 8181
www.jumeirahbeachhotel.com/dining
Richly decorated Lebanese restaurant in landmark hotel. Superb mixed grill. Alcohol. Live music at 10.30pm. Dress: formal. Expensive.

Al Nafoorah
Emirates Towers, Sheikh Zayed Road
Tel: 04 319 8760
www.emiratestowershotel.com/dining
Fine Lebanese in the boulevard area between the two towers. Lunch menu is great value. Pleasant terrace area. Look out for Sheikh Mohammed who drops in from time to time. Alcohol. Dress: smart casual. Moderate.

Automatic
Al Riqqa Road, Deira
Tel: 04 227 7824
Informal Lebanese eatery with pavement seating on an attractive avenue. Fine *mezze* served with fresh vegetables. There's a branch of the same establishment at The Beach Centre in Jumeira (tel: 04 349 4888). Both outlets are virtually always full of diners enjoying unpretentious food, huge servings and generally excellent value for money. No alcohol. Dress: casual. Inexpensive.

Ayam Zamam
Ascot Hotel, Bur Dubai
Tel: 04 352 0900
Highly evocative recreation of the Lebanon of old with waiters in traditional dress, dim, atmospheric lighting and wall carpets. Alcohol (try the *arak* if you dare). *Shisha* pipes available. Live music and belly dancers add to the oriental atmosphere. Dress: smart casual. Moderate.

Tagine
Royal Mirage Hotel, Al Mina Al Siyahi
Tel: 04 399 9999
This sumptuous Moroccan restaurant, located in one of Dubai's leading hotels, recalls the ambience of a bygone, pre-oil age. Excellent food, live music, and alcohol. It is conveniently located near Kasbar nightclub *(see Nightlife, page 76)*. Dress: smart casual. Moderate.

Eastern
Pakistani
Ravi's
Satwa Roundabout, Al Satwa
Tel: 04 331 5353
Ravi's is to Pakistani cuisine what Automatic is to its Arabic equivalent. This is an extremely popular curry house that is set in a thriving neighbourhood, and it has the advantage of an alfresco option of roadside tables for vegetarians. No alcohol. Dress: informal. Inexpensive.

Indian
Chhappan Bhog
Trade Centre Road, Bur Dubai
Tel: 04 396 8176
The North Indian vegetarian meals served here are so delicious that they will appeal to the taste buds of even the most die-hard meateater. Waiters wear traditional Indian clothes. No alcohol. Dress: casual. Inexpensive.

Above: tables on the terrace are always popular

eating out

Coconut Grove
9th Floor, Rydges Plaza Hotel
Tel: 04 398 3800
Serves excellent quality meals in a room that's overflowing with Indian artefacts. Coconut Grove specialises in wonderful spicy curries from south India and Sri Lanka, with Goan influences predominating. Alcohol. Dress: smart casual. Moderate.

Thai
Blue Elephant
Al Bustan Rotana Hotel, Al Garhoud
Tel: 04 282 0000
www.blueelephant.com
Candidate for World's Best Thai Restaurant, with wonderful food and a Thai-village decor that complements the cuisine. Alcohol. Dress: smart casual. Expensive.

Chinese
Golden Dragon
Trade Centre Road, Bur Dubai
Tel: 04 396 7788
A venerable restaurant with Chinese staff and a loyal customer base. Provides fine food in bright, airy surroundings. Recommended for families. No alcohol. Dress: casual. Moderate.

Japanese
Benihana
Al Bustan Rotana Hotel, Al Garhoud
Tel: 04 282 0000
www.benihana.com
Quite small *teppanyaki* and sushi restaurant with an all-you-can-eat sushi and sashimi promotion Tuesday evenings. Minimalist decor. Alcohol. Dress: smart casual. Expensive.

Sho Cho
Dubai Marine Beach Resort, Jumeira
Tel: 04 346 1111
www.dxbmarine.com
Stylish hang-out. Part sushi restaurant, part cocktail bar. Dress: smart casual. Moderate.

Polynesian
Beachcombers
Jumeirah Beach Hotel, Jumeira
Tel: 04 348 0000
www.jumeirahbeachhotel.com/dining
A perfect holiday venue: thatched terrace overlooking the spectacular Burj Al Arab, with good food and a Caribbean band to entertain. Alcohol. Families welcome. Dress: smart casual. Moderate.

Trader Vic's
Crowne Plaza, Sheikh Zayed Road
Tel: 04 305 6399
www.tradervics.com
A happy mishmash of styles – Polynesia meets Asia and the Caribbean. Lively bar with Cuban band and party atmosphere. Quality cocktails. Dress: smart casual. Expensive.

Western
Mediterranean
Focaccia
Hyatt Regency Hotel, Deira
Tel: 04 209 1600
An attractive recreation of a Mediterranean villa, with musicians wandering from room to room. The foccacia, served warm with baked garlic and olive oil, is a treat. Good wine list. Dress: smart casual. Moderate.

European
Verre
Hilton Creek, Deira
Tel: 04 227 1111
www.hiltondubaicreek.com
Restaurant belonging to Gordon Ramsay, the famous UK chef. Minimalist decor; superb food. Highly recommended. Central Dubai. Alcohol. Dress: smart casual. Expensive.

Italian
Da Vinci's
Millennium Airport Hotel, Al Garhoud
Tel: 04 282 3464
Da Vinci's remains popular after moving to a larger venue. It offers the usual Italian staples, represents good value for money and is run by friendly, efficient staff. Alcohol. Dress: smart casual. Moderate.

French
Café Chic
Le Meridien Dubai, Al Garhoud
Tel: 04 702 2455
Elegant and stylish restaurant spread over two levels and serving authentic French food. The desserts, including hot chocolate soufflé, are particularly scrumptious. Alcohol. Dress: smart casual. Expensive.

American
Go West
Jumeirah Beach Hotel, Jumeira
Tel: 04 406 8181
www.jumeirahbeachhotel.com/dining
Great for the family, though the Wild West decor is overpowering. The menu contains all the American favourites, but also more innovative dishes. Dress: casual. Moderate.

JW's Steakhouse
JW Marriott Hotel, Deira
Tel: 04 262 4444
Great grills prepared with an American slant and cooked beneath a flame to your specific taste. Clubby decor that includes lots of panelled wood and deep leather chairs. Good wine list Dress: smart casual. Expensive.

International
The Boardwalk
Dubai Creek Golf & Yacht Club, Al Garhoud
Tel: 04 295 6000
Although the food is good – a selection of salads and oriental dishes, Mexican items and toasted sandwiches – it's the alfresco setting on three large wooden tiers over the Creek that makes The Boardwalk so special. This is the place to watch *dhows*, *abras* and yachts pass by as the sun goes down. Alcohol. Dress: smart casual. Moderate.

Al Dawaar
Hyatt Regency Hotel, Deira
Tel: 04 209 1100
Dubai's only revolving restaurant is on the hotel's 25th floor, and has amazing views north towards Sharjah and, in the opposite direction, to the Creek mouth, Al Shindagha and Port Khalid. An international buffet complements the visual feast. Alcohol. Dress: smart casual. Moderate.

Fish
The Marina Seafood Market
Jumeirah Beach Hotel, Jumeira
Tel: 04 406 8181
The setting – a few hundred metres/yards from Burj Al Arab, on an island linked by causeway to Jumeirah Beach Hotel, accessible by golf cart – is pure James Bond fantasy. There is a wonderful view from the open-air bar, and excellent fish dishes on

the menu. Alcohol. Dress: the word is smart very smart. Expensive.

Fish Bazaar
Metropolitan Hotel, Sheikh Zayed Road
Tel: 04 407 6867
www.methotels.com
Choose your fish and have it cooked to your specifications. Pleasant dining room with view over highway to Abu Dhabi and across Al Safa Park. Alcohol. Dress: casual. Moderate

Friday Brunch
Global Family Brunch (Fontana)
Al Bustan Rotana Hotel, Al Garhoud
Tel: 04 705 4818
The lobby and ground-floor Fontana restaurant of the appealing Al Bustan Rotana Hotel opens for three hours between noon and 3pm on Fridays (the local weekend) for prix-fixe buffet lunches. A very wide choice of cuisine features Arabic, Thai, Japanese, Indian and Italian fare from the hotel's assorted outlets. Alcohol. Entertainment for children. Dress: casual. Moderate.

Others
For both a good dinner and a pleasant evening out, you should definitely consider Century Village, a group of restaurants in a pleasant landscaped setting at the tennis stadium in Al Garhoud. For lunch, the food courts of Dubai's shopping malls can be a convenient option. The Bur Juman Centre on Trade Centre Road in Bur Dubai has one of the best.

If you are travelling with children, there are lots of activities around the food courts of both Deira City Centre and Lamcy Plaza. Elsewhere in City Centre, you might enjoy the Californian-style Coco's restaurant, which has a sister outlet on Sheikh Zayed Road. Also on Sheikh Zayed Road is the very popular Shakespeare & Co restaurant, occupying a corner of Kendah House and the patio outside, and serving wholesome Moroccan and international dishes.

For a traditional snack try a between-meals *zatar* – Arabic bread with thyme, sesame seeds and olive oil. *Zatar* is best eaten straight from the oven at one of the numerous Lebanese bakeries in Deira, Bur Dubai and Jumeira.

Right: after a long day's rest and relaxation, take in the Jumeiran sunset

NIGHTLIFE

You would probably expect a young, dynamic and affluent city to have a thriving social scene, but the fact that Dubai lies in the Muslim Middle East does make its vibrant nightlife somewhat surprising. But as in many western countries, the highly charged private-sector employees behind the surging economy like to spend lavish amounts of their disposable incomes on letting their hair down.

In Dubai you'll find a choice of bars and nightclubs comparable to that in a western city of similar size. True, these are mostly mainstream venues for clean-living expats, but if they satisfy the R&R requirements of party-loving residents, then they should meet with the approval all but the most die-hard of holiday ravers.

Dubai's convivial bars stay open until the wee hours. For obvious reasons there's no indigenous bar culture to build on, so nightlife venues can at first feel like surreal imports. But their vibrancy is undeniable, and they give a good indication of the sheer excitement that comes from living a sun-drenched, beach-side life supported by highly lucrative oil wells.

Not that it's all hectic partying. Western culture is represented by the live events, from concerts to theatrical productions, that take place throughout the cooler months (November–April). All of these events, however, are staged by visiting groups, so they tend to be rather sporadic. And don't rule out a trip to the movies: the latest Hollywood (and for that matter Indian Bollywood) blockbusters are screened in cinemas that have state-of-the-art sound systems.

You should take note of the following three considerations before you embark on a voyage of discovery among Dubai's most popular nocturnal haunts. Firstly, don't be put off by the 'Members Only' signs at some venues – they represent nothing more than management efforts to ensure the right mix of clients. Secondly, belly-dancing is rarer than you might think. Finally, there is virtually no nightlife during the holy month of Ramadan, so before you visit Dubai, check when Ramadan falls.

Bars

The Irish Village (11am–2am) built into the side of Dubai Tennis Stadium in Al Garhoud is a rare gem – a pub that's not associated with a hotel and at which it's possible to enjoy an alfresco drink. And it has live music and a duck pond. Another Irish bar, Dubliner's (11am–1am) serves Irish grub and shows sports events on a big screen. It is located in Le Meridien hotel, Al Garhoud.

For a classier night out, you could try Carter's (noon–2am), which presents a theme of colonial Egypt in the spectacular Pyramids complex at Wafi City. The terrace, decorated to give a subtle 'inside-outside' feel, is an excellent spot in which to relax, but you will have to arrive early to get a candlelit table.

Comparable to Carter's are two other Wafi venues, Seville's Spanish tapas bar (4pm–midnight) and the Asian cocktail bar Ginseng (7pm–2am); and QD's (5pm–1am),

which is an open-air bar on the Creekside next to the Boardwalk at Dubai Creek Golf & Yacht Club. Also worth visiting is the Polynesian Trader Vic's (7.30pm–1am) on the third floor of the Crowne Plaza on Sheikh Zayed Road, which specialises in cocktails and has superb live music.

Dubai's Tex Mex restaurants each have separate bar areas. Pancho Villa's (7pm–2am) in the Astoria Hotel, Bur Dubai, is the most popular *(see Itinerary 1, page 28)*, while The Alamo (7pm–00.45) at Dubai Marine Beach Resort & Spa in Jumeira has live music. Cactus Cantina (noon–11pm), though, has the best view – from the eighth floor of the Rydges Plaza Hotel in Satwa.

Lively bars include Billy Blues (6pm–2am) at the Rydges Plaza; Henry J Beans (noon–2am) just down Al Dhiyafah Road in the Capitol Hotel; Scarlett's (noon–3am) at Emirates Towers; Long's Bar (noon–11.45pm) at the Towers Rotana on Sheikh Zayed Road; and Rock Bottom Café (6pm–3.30am) on Trade Centre Road – the nearest thing in Dubai to an American biker bar. Dubai's Hard Rock Café is a considerable drive out of town on the Abu Dhabi Road. Aussie Legends (3pm–3am) at the Rydges Plaza and Champions (midnight–2am) at the JW Marriott in Deira are popular sports bars.

The Agency (12.30pm–1am) at Emirates Towers is considered the best wine bar in town. On the 51st floor of the nearby hotel tower, Vu's bar (7–11pm) offers an unforgetable perspective on the city. Jazz fans will doubtless appreciate the Inter-Continental Up On The Tenth jazz bar (6.30pm–2.30am), which offers superb views of the Creek. In the same league is the Uptown piano bar (6pm–2am) on the 24th floor of the Jumeirah Beach Hotel, which has another fantastic view.

Nightclubs

A hot spot with apparent staying power is the up-market Planetarium (10pm–3am except Mon) at Planet Hollywood. The Kasbah (10pm–3am except Sun), with its Arabian-theme, at the Royal Mirage Hotel in Al Mina Al Siyahi, has amazing décor and is very popular with a cross-section of locals, expats and visitors.

In Jumeira, Tropicana (7.30pm–3am) at the Dubai Marine Beach Resort & Spa is a great place to dance to Arabian music alongside hip expats from the Levant. Also worth a look is Savage Garden (6pm–3am) at Satwa's Capitol Hotel (excellent Latin music and dance). Fashion tip: don't wear jeans and sneakers.

Live Entertainment

Simply Red, Bryan Adams, James Brown, Sting, Elton John and Chuck Berry are just some of the acts that have all performed in Dubai in recent years. On the dramatic stage, The Reduced Shakespeare Company has staged plays here, and London's Regent's Park Open-Air Theatre Company is an annual visitor. The British Airways Playhouse – starring a number of British household names – frequently appears at the Inter-Con, and visiting comedians take on hecklers at the Hyatt Regency's Laughter Factory.

To find out about upcoming events, you should check the listings in *Time Out Dubai* or *What's On* magazine or consult the *Out & About* free guide. It is also worth tuning in to the English-language radio stations – Dubai FM on 92Mhz, 104.8 Channel Four FM, or Emirates Radio Network 1 and 2, on 104FM and 99.3FM respectively.

Cinema

For listings of films in English, Arabic and Hindi, see the Wednesday 'Entertainment' supplement in *Gulf News*. The best cinemas for western movies are the multi-screen Grand Cineplex in Umm Hurair and Cinestar at Deira City Centre.

Shisha Cafés

Smoking a *shisha* or 'hubble-bubble' pipe as one is popularly known, can be an enjoyable experience, even for non-smokers. The smoke from the strawberry- or apple- or liquorice- flavoured tobacco is drawn from the top of the free-standing *shisha* through water before it reaches you via a long flexible pipe, resulting in a pleasant mild high. You can have a smoke at Mazaj (noon–3am) at Century Village, or the very popular Café Renoir (8.30am–midnight) at Wafi Shopping Mall.

CALENDAR OF EVENTS

January

Dubai Shopping Festival (DSF): a month-long, city-wide festival with discounts at participating outlets, hotels and on air fares. There are heritage and entertainment events, funfairs and pyrotechnic shows daily on the Creek. At night, bright lights transform the city into a giant theme park. DSF is a great time to visit. Find details in *Gulf News* or *Khaleej Times*.

February

Dubai Tennis Championships, Dubai Tennis Stadium, Aviation Club, Al Garhoud: since this US$1 million event's inception in 1993, the biggest names in men's tennis – Edberg, Becker, Muster, Lendl – have played at the purpose-built stadium. In 2001, the event became a two-week festival of tennis featuring the top women, whose WTA tour competition is now staged back to back with the ATP. Hingis, Seles and Venus Williams have all competed in Dubai. Matches take place in afternoons and evenings beginning in the second week of February. Buy tickets on the day or in advance from the sales office in the stadium's north stand.

March

European PGA Dubai Desert Classic, Dubai Creek Golf & Yacht Club or Emirates Golf Club (varies): golf championship contested by many of the world's top players including Tiger Woods and Ernie Els. The Desert Classic takes place every spring, in recent years in March.

Dubai World Cup, Nad Al Sheba: this horse-race meeting is the social highlight of the year and, with US$15 million at stake. Traditionally held in the last week of March, the 2,000-m (10-furlong) title race attracts thoroughbreds from the USA, UK, France, Australia and Japan, jockeys such as America's Jerry Bailey (a two-time winner) and the legendary Frankie Dettori, and crowds of 35,000. Admission to the public enclosure is free; to fully enjoy the day, buy a badge to the International Village from Dubai World Cup (tel: 04 332 2277) in advance. One to dress up for – the ladies' hats are of Ascot proportions.

October – November

UIM Class One World Offshore power-boat championships (final rounds) in the waters off Le Meridien Al Mina Al Siyahi: local interest in the event, which takes place over two weekends in late October/early November, focuses on frequent world champions, the Dubai-based Victory team.

UAE Desert Challenge: a World Cup car and motorbike rally that takes place largely in the desert between Abu Dhabi and Dubai, usually with a stage in a city venue. Locals support Middle East champion Mohammed Bin Sulayem. For details, see the local press, or call the organisers (tel: 04 266 9922).

Dubai Airshow: biennial (odd-number years) extravaganza, a trade event that's closed to the public. From the streets around Dubai International Airport, you can see the afternoon flying displays by formation teams such as Britain's Red Arrows. The gala dinner is invitation-only, but the post-dinner concert is open to the public.

December

National Day: a three-day holiday in the first week of December marks the founding of the UAE in 1971. Parks and public places host cultural activities such as folk dancing, and at night the city is festooned in decorative lights. Celebrations include the two-day **Dubai Rugby Sevens** tournament at Dubai Exiles Rugby Club near Bu Kidra interchange. Matches start at 9.30am and continue until the late evening. Daily and season tickets are available at the gate.

Right: dancers at Creekside Park

Practical Information

GETTING THERE

By Air

The main gateway is Dubai International Airport (tel: 04 224 5555; www.dubaiairport.com), which is minutes away from downtown Deira. Having undergone a US$540 million expansion, this bustling Middle East passenger and cargo hub has a futuristic new terminal and air traffic control tower, and an even larger Dubai Duty Free.

The home of the award-winning national carrier Emirates, Dubai airport is served by the major airlines and global alliance partners of Europe and Asia – British Airways, Lufthansa, KLM, Air France, Swissair, PIA, Air India, Singapore Airlines, Malaysia, Thai and Cathay Pacific among them.

Malaysia (www.malaysiaairlines.com) has until recently provided the only direct flight to and from the United States, but Emirates (www.emirates.com) – whose network extends as far as South Africa and Australia – now also flies direct to New York. The flight time to Dubai from Europe is around seven hours, or 13 hours from New York. There's no airport departure tax on leaving Dubai.

TRAVEL ESSENTIALS

When to Visit

November to April is the time when the climate, and indeed the sports and social scenes, are at their best. Before you book, it's advisable to check when the Holy Month of Ramadan falls, as this leads to certain restrictions, particularly on nightlife.

Visas and Passports

Visas are required by all nationalities except GCC members. Citizens of the UK, USA, Canada, Australia and most West European and Far Eastern countries are entitled to an automatic free visit visa on entry, while other nationalities should obtain business, tourist or transit visas through UAE embassies abroad or via the UAE hotel they have booked with. If you opt for the latter, you'll be under the hotel's sponsorship and are obliged to stay there for at least a few nights.

Vaccinations

No special injections are required prior to visiting the UAE.

Customs

The duty-free allowances are as follows: 2,000 cigarettes, 400 cigars or 2kg loose tobacco, and – for non-Muslims – 2 litres of wine and spirits. There are no limits on perfume. DVDs and video cassettes may be confiscated on arrival but can be retrieved once their content has been checked.

Weather

Summers are very hot and humid. From May to September daytime temperatures are rarely below 40°C (104°F) with humidity up to 90 per cent. From October to April the weather resembles an exceptionally good European summer, with temperatures hovering around 30°C (mid-80s°F) and little or no humidity.

Evenings can feel a little chilly around January/February and jumpers may be required. Annual rainfall is minimal (an average of 42mm), but downpours occur January to March; when it rains, it pours. Inland, Hatta is a little cooler, particularly at night in winter.

Left: Deira's Twin Towers
Right: waiting for a joyrider

Clothing

Comfortable loose cottons suit the climate best, with peak caps or sun hats for protection during the heat of the day. In terms of culture, while the most daring swimwear is acceptable on the beach, around town visitors should be more modest and avoid wearing very short shorts and dresses and tight tops. Outside Dubai, more care should be taken to avoid showing too much bare skin: everyone's upper arms should be covered, and women are advised to wear long skirts or trousers.

Electricity

220/240 volts, 50 cycles AC. British-style three-pin sockets are common. Adaptors can be bought from Carrefour hypermarket at Deira City Centre.

Weights and Measures

Metric.

Time Differences

GMT + 4 hours, BST + 3 hours.

GETTING ACQUAINTED

Geography

Dubai is the second city (after Abu Dhabi) of the United Arab Emirates (UAE) and the capital of Dubai emirate, which covers some 3,900 sq km (1,506 miles). It is situated on the Arabian Gulf coast, on the eastern edge of the Arabian peninsula and was built around a wide waterway, or creek.

Dubai city is flat and bordered on three sides by desert. Inland, at Hatta, the Hajar Mountains begin their ascent to a peak of 2,000m (6,560ft), as they separate the Gulf emirates from the Arabian Sea. To the south of the UAE lies Saudi Arabia, while Oman – just over an hour's drive from Dubai – lies to the east.

Government and Economy

The UAE is a federation of seven emirates, all of which are ruled by sheikhs. The president of the UAE is the ruler of Abu Dhabi, the federal capital, Sheikh Zayed Bin Sultan Al Nahyan. The ruler of Dubai, Sheikh Maktoum Bin Rashid Al Maktoum, is the vice president and prime minister of the UAE. Sheikh Maktoum's brother, Sheikh Mohammed Bin Rashid Al Maktoum, is the crown prince of Dubai and also the UAE's minister of defence. The federal government runs a major part of the country's infrastructure and affairs, while the individual emirates retain considerable autonomy.

The UAE economy is based on oil and gas extraction, which forms about 40 percent of GDP. In recent years, the importance of non-oil industries has been recognised. Tourism in particular is undergoing a boom, with the number of visitors to Dubai rising from 1.8 million in 1997 to more than 3 million in 2000.

Religion

Islam is the official religion of Dubai. UAE nationals are Sunni Muslims. Other religions are tolerated.

How Not to Offend

Dubai is one of the more liberal Gulf cities and nationals are both familiar with and reasonably tolerant of those from other cultures. Even so, any extra effort to respect Arab sensibilities is greatly appreciated.

Some don'ts:

Don't try and rush things, particularly with officialdom, which likes to take its time even over matters of apparent urgency – patience is a virtue; don't photograph nationals without first asking their permission; don't stare at national women, though the temptation is sometimes great; don't offer alcohol to Muslims; don't show the soles of your feet when sitting among nationals; don't eat, drink or smoke in public areas during the Holy Month of Ramadan – the penalties are severe; never drink and drive.

And some dos:

Do dress modestly away from the beach; and if time permits do graciously accept any hospitality that's offered – a refusal would be considered rude.

Population

Curiously, it's possible to visit Dubai and not meet a national except for those at the airport immigration counter, the post office or the bank.

The UAE's population may be rising to the 3 million mark (around 1 million of whom live in Dubai), but around 70 percent of that total are expatriates. Asian immigrants account for the bulk of these, and you're likely to hear Hindi, Urdu, Malayalam and Tagalog as much as – if not more than – Arabic.

Hours and Holidays

Business Hours

Although it varies, particularly in the Westernised private sector, the working week is generally from Saturday to Thursday lunchtime, with Friday off.

Government offices work from 7 or 7.30am–1.30pm Saturday to Wednesday. On Thursday, offices tend to close for the weekend at noon.

Banks, private companies and shops typically open 8 or 9am–1/1.30pm and 4/4.30–

8pm Saturday to Wednesday, closing at 1.30pm on Thursday. Increasingly, the larger shopping malls open from 10am–10pm Saturday to Thursday and on Friday from around 2pm to late evening.

Public Holidays

Religious holidays are governed by the Islamic (Hegira) calendar and therefore do not fall on fixed dates. The main holidays are as follows:

Eid Al Fitr (the end of Ramadan); *Eid Al Adha* (during the month of the Haj, or pilgrimage to Mecca); the ascension of the Prophet; the Prophet's birthday; and Islamic New Year.

Other public holidays (*see Calendar of Events, page 77*) are New Year's Day (1 January) and National Day (2–3 December).

MONEY MATTERS

Currency

The UAE dirham (abbreviated to AED or Dhs). One dirham is 100 fils and value linked to the US dollar at Dhs 3.67.

Credit Cards

Major cards such as Visa, Mastercard, American Express and Diners Club are widely accepted in hotels, restaurants and shops.

Left: local girls enjoying a celebration at Creekside Park
Above: a porter waits

However, if you plan to bargain, it's better to have cash.

Cash Machines
There are globally linked ATM points at banks, shopping malls and some hotels.

Traveller's Cheques
Sometimes accepted in major shops, but generally not a useful cash equivalent. However, TCs can easily be exchanged at banks and money changers.

Money Changers
More convenient than banks in terms of opening hours and their location in busy shopping areas, money changers offer varying rates that are sometimes better than banks. All currencies accepted.

Tipping
It's not compulsory but most people do tip, even in restaurants where a service charge has been added to the bill. Ten percent should suffice. Supermarket employees who pack and carry bags and petrol pump attendants who clean windscreens are also tipped, but in coins rather than notes.

Taxes
A tax and service charge of between 15 and 20 percent is sometimes added to hotel bills. Check that this is included in prices quoted.

GETTING AROUND

Taxi
This is the best way to get around the city. Dubai Transport Corporation or DTC (tel: 04 208 0808) operates the ubiquitous light mustard-coloured cabs, which are metered, air-conditioned, clean and reliable. The fare from the airport is higher than from elsewhere in the city but generally taxis are considerably cheaper than taxis in western cities. In fact, the fare often equates to that of a bus or tube in London. Other metered cabs are operated by Metro Taxis (tel: 04 267 3222) and National Taxis (tel: 04 336 6611).

Left: one hump or two?

Non-metered cabs offer the best value for long (shared) trips to other cities. Such 'service taxis' for Sharjah and the Northern Emirates leave from Deira Taxi Station near the Al Ghurair Centre, while those for Abu Dhabi and Al Ain run from the Al Ghubabiba Bus and Taxi Station in Bur Dubai.

A word of warning:
Taxi drivers often don't know Dubai as well as you would probably expect, so, if you can, direct them.

Bus
Used mainly by low-income workers, Dubai's bus service – which operates in Deira from Al Sabkha Bus Station between the Gold Souk and Beniyas Square, and in Bur Dubai from Al Ghubaiba Street – is not a suitable alternative to taxis for trips within the city. However, for longer journeys a bus can offer both a money-saving alternative to rental cars and an experience to remember. The bus for Hatta is the No 16.

Water Taxi
By far the best way to appreciate the Creek and sample the bustle of daily life in the heart of the old city is to take a water taxi, or *abra*. Fares are just 50 fils for trips from Bur Dubai to Deira and vice versa, but for Dhs 50 an *abra* captain would be happy to take you as far as Maktoum Bridge or beyond. For further details about water taxis and the various embarkation points, *see Itinerary 1, page 26.*

Car
For a city that didn't have a single stretch of tarmac when oil was discovered, Dubai's road infrastructure is excellent. All the major car rental agencies have offices in Dubai. To get a temporary driving licence, just hand over your passport, national or international driving licence and two photographs and the agency will arrange the paperwork.

Among the international hire companies are Avis (tel: 04 295 7121), Budget (tel: 04 282 3030), Hertz (tel: 04 282 4422) and Thrifty (tel: 04 224 5404). Remember to drive on the right, always carry your licence with you and never drink and drive. Speed limits are normally between 60 kph (37 mph) and 100 kph (62 mph).

ACCOMMODATION

Hotels

Dubai's hotels range from the ordinary to the extraordinary. You should be aware that the most luxurious hotels open their visitor attractions to nonresidents.

Generally, hotels in Dubai – as in the rest of the UAE – are not cheap; they tend to cater for tour groups and business people on the international meetings, conferences and exhibitions circuit rather than to independent budget travellers. The best deals are likely to be found through tour operators, though furnished apartments are an economical alternative.

The majority of less expensive hotels can be found in Bur Dubai and Deira, while – with a few notable exceptions – the most desirable establishments are on the Arabian Gulf coast. Stretching from Jumeira through Umm Suqeim to Al Mina Al Siyahi, the coast is commonly referred to as 'Jumeira'. Although Jumeira may seem some distance from the airport on maps, the hotels in this neighbourhood are actually a mere 30 minutes' drive away.

If you choose to book into a landlocked hotel in the city, check to see whether it has a sister hotel on the coast which will have beachside facilities that you are entitled to use; among those that do are Le Meridien Dubai, which is situated conveniently close to the airport, and The Metropolitan Hotel on the Dubai–Abu Dhabi highway (Sheikh Zayed Road).

For convenience, the following listings are alphabetical under the headings 'Coastal Hotels', 'City Hotels South of the Creek', 'City Hotels North of the Creek' and 'Outside Dubai'.

The price indicators after each listing are based on the following:
$ = $75–150 per room
$$ = $150–225 per room
$$$ $225–300 per room
$$$$ = £300 plus.

The best deals are available during the northern hemisphere's summer months. To find out about Dubai's hotels on the web, visit *www.asiatravel.com/uae*

Coastal Hotels

Burj al Arab
PO Box 74147
Tel: 04 301 7777, fax: 04 301 7001
www.burj-al-arab.com
The tallest all-suite hotel in the world, built on its own island off The Jumeirah Beach Hotel, Burj Al Arab offers the utmost in luxury accommodation. Each duplex has a laptop computer, 114-cm (45-inch) television, Italian marble, Irish linen and bedroom ceiling mirrors. Guests are ferried around in a fleet of eight white Rolls-Royces. A one-bedroom duplex will set you back Dhs 3,500 (£603) per night plus 20 percent tax/service charge. *$$$$*

Above: the Royal Mirage Hotel

Dubai Marine Beach Resort and Spa
PO Box 5182,
Beach Road, Jumeira
Tel: 04 346 1111, fax: 04 346 0234
www.dubaimarine.com
The nearest beach resort facility to downtown Dubai, this 195-room complex has a small private beach, two pools, a spa and a selection of popular restaurants. *$$*

The Jumeirah Beach Hotel
PO Box 11416,
Tel: 04 3480 000, fax: 04 348 2273
www.jumeirahinternational.com
Voted the number one hotel in the world by readers of Conde Naste's *Traveller* magazine in 1999, the 26-storey Jumeirah Beach is designed to look like a wave to complement Burj Al Arab's 'sail'. It has 600 sea-facing rooms, a breathtaking atrium and a whole town's worth of restaurants and bars. *$$$$*

Le Royal Meridien Beach Resort & Spa
PO Box 24970
Al Sufouh Road, Jumeira
Tel: 04 399 5555, fax: 04 399 5999
www.meridien.com
A family favourite, with lush lawns leading to a stunning beach and a wonderful pool bar that also serves good quality lunches. Beach facilities can also be used by non-residents for a reasonable daily fee. The Fusion restaurant is one of the best in town. *$$$*

The Metropolitan Resort & Beach Club
PO Box 24454, Jumeira
Tel: 04 399 5000, fax: 04 399 4547
email: metbeach@emirates.net.ae
Not the most impressive hotel on the Jumeira coast but a five-star hotel nonetheless with beachside facilities that include a waterslide. Sister to the Metropolitan Palace and Metropolitan Hotel. *$$$$*

Oasis Beach Hotel
PO Box 26500,
off Al Sufouh Road, Jumeira
Tel: 04 399 4444
Fax: 04 399 4200
www.hfh@jaihotels.com
The Oasis has a very pleasant beachfront, with large terrace, pool bar, lawns and beach, as well as the high level of service expected of a sister to the Jebel Ali and Hatta Fort hotels. Good value. *$$*

Ritz-Carlton Dubai
PO Box 26525,
Off Al Sufouh Road, Jumeira
Tel: 04 399 4000, fax: 04 399 4001
www.ritzcarlton.com/resorts/dubai/
Probably one of the top three hotels in Dubai, the elegant, Spanish-influenced Ritz-Carlton has only 138 rooms and doesn't attract the large numbers of non-residents who flock to the Jumeirah Beach Hotel. As a result, it's a quieter holiday haven. Ideal for couples. *$$$$*

Royal Mirage
PO Box 37252,
Al Sufouh Road, Al Mina Al Siyahi, Jumeira
Tel: 04 399 9999, fax: 04 399 9998
www.oneandonly.com
One of Dubai's best hotels, a 250-room resort with fabulous decor, lush oasis greenery, superb restaurants and an 'in' nightspot, the Kasbar. One for romantics. *$$$$*

Sheraton Jumeira Beach Resort
PO Box 53567, Jumeira
Tel: 04 399 5533, fax: 04 399 5577
www.starwood.com/sheraton
Although it's close to an industrial area north of Jebel Ali port, this southernmost of Jumeira hotels retains unspoilt views of the Gulf and is very popular with cabin crews, among others. *$$$*

City Hotels – South of the Creek

Crowne Plaza Dubai
PO Box 23215, Sheikh Zayed Road
Tel: 04 331 1111, fax: 04 331 5555
www.dubai.crowneplaza.com
Set at the Satwa end of Sheikh Zayed Road, this is a good base for exploring Dubai south of the creek, particularly if you're renting a car; Jumeira and Nad Al Sheba are minutes away. The hotel's Trader Vic's is a local hot spot, the bars of Satwa are nearby. *$$$$*

Dusit Dubai
PO Box 23335, Sheikh Zayed Road
Tel: 04 343 3333, fax: 04 343 3352
www.dusit.com
Futuristic Thai-owned hotel and a Sheikh Zayed Road landmark. *$$$$*

Emirates Towers Hotel
PO Box 72127, Sheikh Zayed Road
Tel: 04 330 0000, fax: 04 330 3131
www.emiratestowershotel.com
Situated next to the World Trade Centre. One of the tallest hotels in the world, with a good range of rooms at various price levels and lovely landscaped grounds.
$$–$$$$

Fairmont Hotel
PO Box 97555, Sheikh Zayed Road
Tel: 04 332 5555, fax: 04 332 4555
www.fairmont.com
The Canadian chain's first venture outside North America. A very distinctive building topped by four pyramids. The space-age interior boasts several fashionable venues for those who like to be seen.
$$$$

Grand Hyatt
PO Box 7978, Umm Hurair
Tel: 04 317 1234, fax: 04 317 1235
www.dubai.grand.hyatt.com
One of Dubai's newest hotels. 674 rooms and quality suites in a central location near Wafi City.
$$$$

The Metropolitan Hotel
PO Box 26666, Sheikh Zayed Road
Tel: 04 343 0000, fax: 04 343 1146
www.methotels.com
Just across the Dubai–Abu Dhabi Highway from Safa Park and not far from Nad Al Sheba Racecourse.
$$$$

Ramada Hotel
PO Box 7979,
Al Mankhool Road, Bur Dubai
Tel: 04 351 9999, fax: 04 352 1033
www.ramadadubai.com
The Ramada is within walking distance of the Creek, the old Bastakia district, Dubai Museum, Dubai Old Souk and the Bur Juman Centre. Also convenient for the thriving nightlife scene in the area.
$$

Towers Rotana
PO Box 30430, Sheikh Zayed Road

Tel: 04 343 8000, fax: 04 343 5111
www.rotana.com
Smart business hotel with great evening venues such as Long's Bar and the Teatro restaurant.
$$$

City Hotels – North of the Creek

Al Bustan Rotana
PO Box 30880, Al Garhoud
Tel: 04 282 0000, fax: 04 282 8100
www.rotana.com
The light, airy and spacious foyer – where there's a relaxing Global Family Brunch buffet on Fridays – immediately sets the tone. Classy and spacious, the Al Bustan is very convenient for the airport and the Irish Village at Dubai Tennis Stadium.
$$$

Hilton Creek
PO Box 33398, Deira
Tel: 227 1111, fax: 227 1131
www.hiltondubai.com
Chic business hotel designed by Carlos Ott and boasting Gordon Ramsay's Verre restaurant. *$$$$*

Hotel Inter-Continental Dubai
PO Box 476, Bani Yas Road, Deira
Tel: 04 222 7171, fax: 04 223 7615
www.ichotelsgroup.com
Possibly the best city-centre hotel with views of Dubai Creek, the Inter-Con is an excellent base from which to explore the souks of Deira and the boutiques of nearby Al Riqqa and Al Maktoum Roads.
$$$$

Right: Al Bustan Rotana Hotel employee

Hyatt Regency Dubai
PO Box 5588, Corniche Street, Deira
Tel: 04 209 1234
Fax: 04 209 1235
www.dubai.hyatt.com
An imposing monolith dominating the mouth of Dubai Creek, the Hyatt Regency is one of the city's liveliest hotels, boasting excellent restaurants (a visit to Focaccia is a must), a cinema and even an ice-rink. The closest quality hotel to Dubai's Gold Souk. *$$$$*

JW Marriott Hotel
PO Box 16590,
Abu Baker Al Siddique Road, Deira
Tel: 04 262 4444, fax: 04 262 6264
www.marriott.com
In the heart of Deira, on the road that leads to Clock Tower Roundabout and Al Maktoum Bridge, the recently enlarged Marriott might not front on to a beach but it nonetheless draws large crowds attracted to outlets such as the Italian Cucina, JW's Steakhouse and the popular Champions sports bar. *$$$*

The Metropolitan Palace Hotel
PO Box 56262,
Al Maktoum Street, Deira
Tel: 04 2270 000, fax: 04 227 9993
www.methotels.com
This is where Hollywood's A list stars chose to stay for the opening of Dubai's Planet Hollywood restaurant in 1998. The Metropolitan Palace is an elegant hotel that compensates for its land-locked position with Central Park-style sophistication. It's sister to the Metropolitan Hotel on Sheikh Zayed Road and the Metropolitan Resort & Beach Club in Jumeira. *$$$$*

The Millennium Airport Hotel
PO Box 13018, Al Garhoud
Tel: 04 282 3464, fax: 04 282 3781
www2.millenniumhotels.com
Among a cluster of Al Garhoud hotels that include Le Meridien Dubai and the Al Bustan Rotana, the Airport Hotel offers outstanding value for money. It's convenient for the Dubai Tennis Stadium complex, Deira and – as the name suggests – the airport. Expanded in 2000, the hotel has an Italian restaurant, Da Vinci's, that's one of the best in town. *$*

Ramada Continental
PO Box 31999, Hor Al Anz
Tel: 04 266 2666, fax: 04 266 8887
www.ramadacontinental.com
On Abu Hail Road, in the northern Hor Al Anz district, a long way from the Creek and Jumeira. On the plus side, it's convenient for Al Mamzar Beach Park. The Cricketers' sports bar broadcasts major sports events and has live music most nights. *$$*

The Renaissance Dubai
PO Box 8668, Salah Al Din Road, Deira
Tel: 04 262 5555, fax: 04 269 7358
www.marriott.com
On busy Salah Al Din Road in the heart of Deira. Its Spice Island 'all you can eat' restaurant is one of Dubai's best. *$$$*

Sheraton Deira
PO Box 5772, Al Mateena Street, Deira
Tel: 04 268 8888, fax: 04 268 8876
www.sheraton.com
Set in Deira's backstreets, away from Dubai Creek, the Sheraton Deira offers the all the comforts expected of the global chain. *$$$$*

Sheraton Dubai Creek Hotel and Towers
PO Box 4250, Beniyas Road, Deira
Tel: 04 228 1111, fax: 04 221 3468
www.sheraton.com
A veritable old-timer of 20 years' standing, this five-star hotel occupies a prime position on Dubai Creek near the Dubai Chamber of Commerce and the *dhow* quays. *$$$*

Sofitel City Centre Hotel
PO Box 61871, City Centre, Deira
Tel: 04 294 1222, fax: 04 295 5544
www.sofitel.com
A business hotel and residence, City Centre is just a short distance from Dubai Creek Golf & Yacht Club. Near the convergence of several highways in Deira. *$$$*

Outside Dubai

Al Maha Resort
PO Box 7631
Tel: 04 303 4222, fax: 04 343 9696
email: almaha@emirates.com
Meaning 'escape' in Arabic, Al Maha offers the most Arabian accommodation in Dubai without any compromise on luxury.

Not so much a hotel as a desert encampment of 30 luxury chalet 'tents' deep in a large nature reserve, this is the first eco-tourism resort in Dubai. Activities include camel riding, falconery and desert safaris. $$$$

Hatta Fort Hotel
PO Box 9277, Hatta
Tel: 852 3211, fax: 852 3561
www.hfh@jaihotels.com
Around an hour's drive from Dubai and set in 32ha (80 acres) of grounds amidst the Hajar Mountains near historic Hatta and the border with Oman, the 50-room Hatta Fort is a popular weekend retreat for city residents. A great base for wadi and desert adventures, the hotel also offers archery and shooting. Outstanding value for money. $

Jebel Ali Hotel & Golf Resort
PO Box 9255, Jebel Ali
Tel: 04 883 6000, fax: 04 883 5543
email: jagrs@jaihotels.com
Set in 50 ha (125 acres) of landscaped gardens, and complete with a nine-hole golf course and an attractive beachfront, the Jebel Ali Hotel is one of the most picturesque hotels on the Gulf, despite its location on the southern boundary of the Jebel Ali Port complex. Although it might be situated too far out of Dubai to be ideal for the avid sightseer, it's only 45 minutes from Dubai airport. Activities include shooting and riding. $$

Other Accommodation
Furnished apartments are centrally located and can offer good value for money, especially when booked from overseas. If you're on limited funds, you might consider combining a stay at one with a night or two at the likes of the Jumeirah Beach Hotel, the Royal Mirage and the Hatta Fort.
Popular choices are:
• Golden Sands III (tel: 04 355 5553; fax: 04 352 6903)
• London Crown Apartments (tel: 04 351 6999; fax: 04 352 9595)
• Dubai Youth Hostel (tel: 04 298 8161; fax: 04 298 8141). This hostel is on Qusais Road on the northern perimeter of the city. Basic accommodation is available for men, women and families, but single women may be refused a booking if the hostel is busy with men.

HEALTH & EMERGENCIES
Hygiene/General Health
Dubai is a modern, clean city. Its public lavatories are well-maintained (the WCs are mostly Western-style) and it's quite okay to drink the tap water – though most residents prefer to drink bottled water, which is an especially advisable practice outside Dubai. One of the most popular brands of bottled water is the locally-produced Masafi.

Pharmacies
To find details of pharmacies that stay open for 24 hours a day consult the listing in the local press or contact the municipality's emergency number (tel: 04 221 5555).

Medical/Dental Services
Healthcare is of a high standard but expensive so it's a good idea to take out travel insurance. There are good government hospitals as well as numerous private clinics. Those that handle emergencies include Al Wasl Hospital (tel: 04 324 1111), the American Hospital (tel: 04 336 7777) and Rashid Hospital (tel: 337 4000).

Dental problems can be dealt with by the American Dental Clinic (tel: 04 344 0668), the Jumeira Beach Dental Clinic (tel: 04 349 9433) or the Swedish Dental Clinic (tel: 04 223 1297).

Crime/Trouble
Dubai is a relatively a safe city. Although petty theft is common, major crimes are rare and the level of personal security is high.

Right: motorcycle traffic cop at Al Shindagha

Many women feel comfortable on their own in the evening. However, while you can let your guard down to some extent, it's best to avoid complacency and take the precautions you'd take anywhere else. .

Police/Fire/Ambulance

As in the UK, the emergency number to call for the police is 999, but ambulances are on 998 and the fire service on 997.

Dubai Police Headquarters can be reached on 04 229 2222.

COMMUNICATIONS & NEWS

Post

Dubai Central Post Office is on Zabeel Road in Karama and there are a number of smaller post offices around town. Poste restante facilities are not available in the UAE.

Telephone

Direct international telephone dialling is available from all phones. Local calls within Dubai are free from a subscriber's phone. You should not have a problem finding coin- and card-operated public telephones on the streets and in shopping malls. Cards can be bought at nearby shops. Hotels tend to charge a premium for calls.

The international dialling code for the UAE is 971. Dubai's city code is 04 (omit the zero when dialling from overseas). US access codes are as follow: AT&T 800 121; MCI WORLDCOM 800111; Sprint 800-131

Internet

The UAE is connected to the world wide web. The sole provider of internet services in the country is the national telecommunications company, Etisalat. Web-based e-mail accounts can be checked at hotel business centres, the Internet Café in the Dune Centre, Satwa (tel: 04 345 3390), Plug-ins Internet Café at Deira's City Centre shopping mall (tel: 04 295 0404), the FI net cafe (tel: 04 345 1461) in the Palm Strip Mall, Jumeira or the two internet cafés on the first floor at Emirates Towers boulevard.

Media

The main English-language newspapers are *Gulf News*, *Khaleej Times* and *The Gulf Today*. The main sources of information on events are *Time Out Dubai* and *What's On*, monthly listings magazines. The free monthly *Out & About* guide contains a useful run-down of current events.

Dubai's English-language TV station is the government-run Dubai Channel 33, which broadcasts evening news bulletins around British and American serials and films. The channel also provides extensive coverage of horse racing. Most hotels and homes also have satellite and cable channels.

Radio is the best medium for getting a feel for Dubai's social scene. The best local English-language radio stations are the government-owned Dubai FM on 92Mhz and the independent Emirates Radio Network 1 and 2, on 104FM and 99.3FM respectively. You'll also be able to pick up 104.8 Channel Four FM from Ajman. The standard is generally high.

USEFUL INFORMATION

Bookshops

The best are Magrudy's Bookshop in Magrudy Shopping Mall on Jumeira's Beach Road and at Deira City Centre, Books Plus in Lamcy Plaza and Book Corner in Deira City Centre and Dar al Hikma, Al Diyafa Street, Statwa.

Left: Internet Café, Satwa

Language

The official language is Arabic, but English is widely spoken and understood.

Sport

Dubai is a sports lover's paradise. There is often a chance to see the world's top sportsmen in action *(see Calendar of Events, page 77)* and strive to emulate them on championship golf courses and hotel tennis courts.

The top 18-hole golf courses are Dubai Creek Golf & Yacht Club (tel: 04 295 6000), Emirates Golf Club (tel: 04 347 3222) and Nad Al Sheba Club (tel: 04 336 3666), at Nad Al Sheba.

Rent jet skis near Al Garhoud Bridge and on the lagoon near Al Mamzar Beach Park; diving tuition can be booked through Emirates Diving Association on 04 393 9390.

Horse riding is available at Emirates Riding Centre (tel: 04 336 1394).

Useful Contacts

Tourist Offices

Dept of Tourism and Commerce Marketing website:www.dubaitourism.co.ae

International Offices:

Australia and New Zealand: Level 6, 75 Miller Street, North Sydney, NSW, Australia 2060 (tel: 00 61 2 9956 6620).
South Africa: PO Box 698, Rivonia 2128, Johannesburg (tel: 00 27 11 785 4600).

UK and Ireland: 125 Pall Mall, London SW1Y 5EA (tel: 00 44 20 7839 0580).
United States: East and Central: 8 Penn Center, Philadelphia, PA 19103 (tel: 00 1 215 751 9750); West Coast: 901 Wilshire Boulevard, Santa Monica, CA 90401 (tel: 00 1 310 752 4488).

Embassies

Australia: Emarat Atrium, Sheikh Zayed Road (tel: 04 321 2444).
France: API World Tower, Sheikh Zayed Road (tel: 04 332 9040).
UK: Al Seef Road, Bur Dubai (tel: 04 397 1070).
United States: Dubai World Trade Centre (tel: 04 311 6000).

FURTHER READING

Insight Guide Oman & The UAE, Editor Dorothy Stannard, APA Publications, 2000.
This Strange Eventful History, Edward Henderson, Motivate. Memoirs of a long-term resident of the UAE. A fascinating and readable account of how the country evolved.
The Trucial States, D. Hawley. An historical perspective by a British ex-diplomat.
Rashid, The Man Behind Dubai, Abbas Abdullah Makki. A very readable memoir of Dubai just before oil was found in quantity.
A History of the Arab People, A. Hourani. Excellent general introduction.

Above: fairways and greens at Dubai Creek Golf & Yacht Club

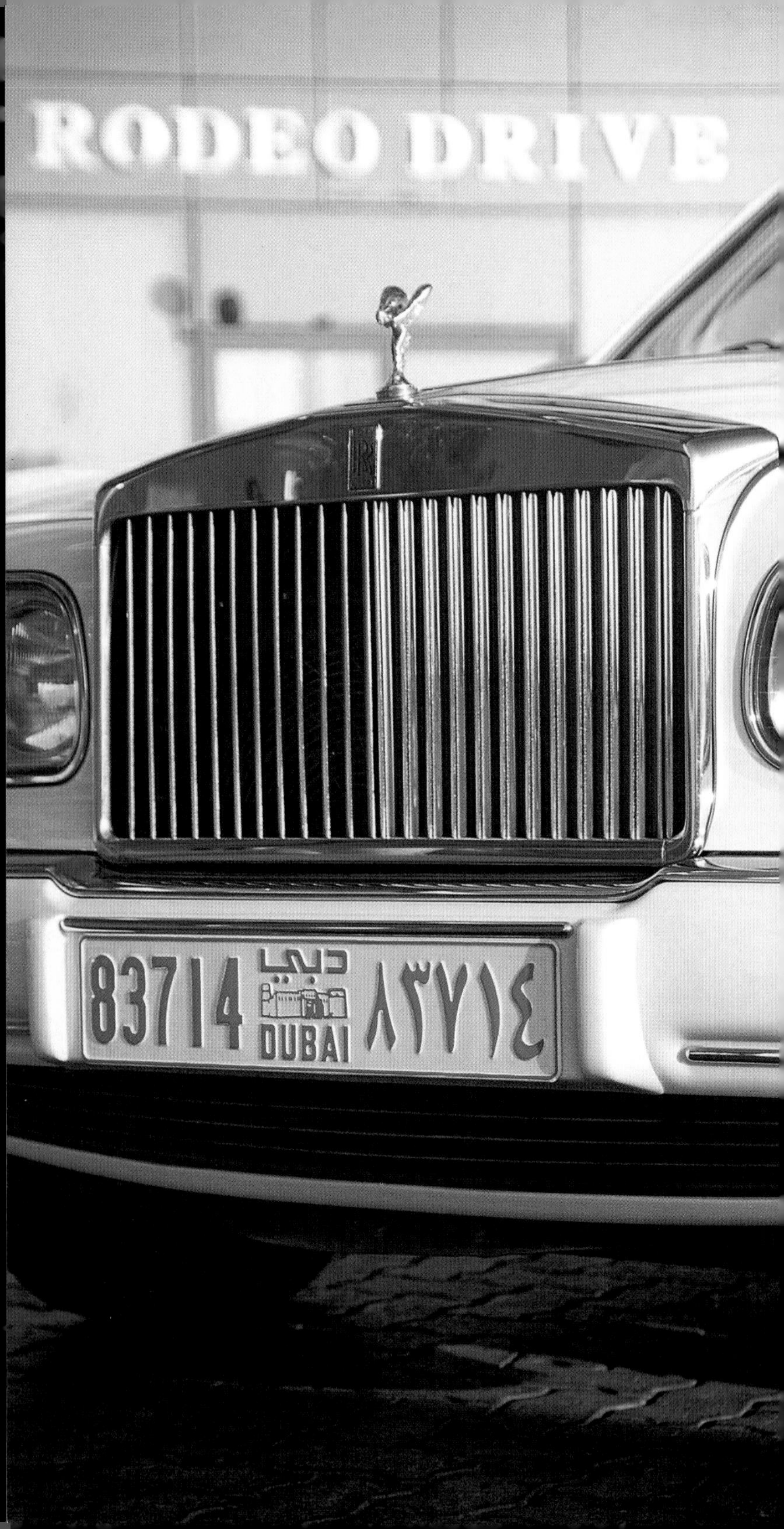
RODEO DRIVE
83714
دبي
DUBAI
٨٣٧١٤

ACKNOWLEDGEMENTS

Photography by	**Matt Jones** *and*
65, 66, 67, 69	**Camerapix/Duncan Willets**
10, 13	**Ronald Codrai**
15	**Ozzie Newcombe**
14	**Topham**
Cover	**Jon Arnold**
Back Cover	**Matt Jones**
Cover Design	**Klaus Geisler**
Cartography	**Berndtson & Berndtson**
Production	**Tanvir Virdee**

Left: the ultimate motor

www.insightguides.com

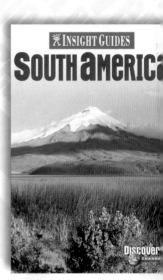

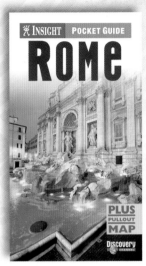
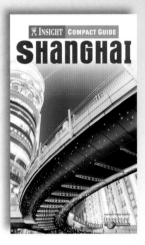

INDEX